ISSUES IN POLITICAL THEORY

Political Theory has undergone a remarkable development in recent years. From a state in which it was once declared dead, it has come to occupy a central place in the study of Politics. Both political ideas and the wide-ranging arguments to which they give rise are now treated in a rigorous, analytical fashion, and political theorists have contributed to disciplines as diverse as economics, sociology and law. These developments have made the subject more challenging and exciting, but they have also added to the difficulties of students and others coming to the subject for the first time. Much of the burgeoning literature in specialist books and journals is readily intelligible only to those who are already well-versed in the subject.

Issues in Political Theory is a series conceived in response to this situation. It consists of a number of detailed and comprehensive studies of issues central to Political Theory which take account of the latest developments in scholarly debate. While making original contributions to the subject, books in the series are written especially for those who are new to Political Theory. Each volume aims to introduce its readers to the intricacies of a fundamental political issue and to help them find their way through the detailed, and often complicated, argument that issue has attracted.

PETER JONES

ALBERT W

ISSUES IN POLITICAL THEORY

Series editors: PETER JONES and ALBERT WEALE

Published

Forthcoming

Series Standing Order

If you would like to receive future titles in this series as they are published, you can make use of our standing order facility. To place a standing order please contact your bookseller or, in case of difficulty, write to us at the address below with your name and address and the name of the series. Please state with which title you wish to begin your standing order. (If you live outside the United Kingdom we may not have the rights for your area, in which case we will forward your order to the publisher concerned.)

Customer Services Department, Macmillan Distribution Ltd
Houndmills, Basingstoke, Hampshire, RG21 2XS, England.

Toleration and the Limits of Liberalism

Susan Mendus

MACMILLAN

First published 1989

Published by
MACMILLAN EDUCATION LTD
Houndmills, Basingstoke, Hampshire RG21 2XS
and London
Companies and representatives
throughout the world

Typeset by Wessex Typesetters
(Division of The Eastern Press Ltd)
Frome, Somerset

Printed in Hong Kong

British Library Cataloguing in Publication Data
Mendus, Susan
Toleration and the limits of liberalism.
1. Toleration
I. Title
179′.9
ISBN 0–333–40405–X (hardcover)
ISBN 0–333–40406–8 (paperback)

For my parents

Contents

Acknowledgements

This book was written during the academic years 1985–7, when I was Morrell Fellow in Toleration at the University of York. Those two years were exceptionally happy ones for me, both professionally and personally. My thanks go to the Trustees of the C. and J. B. Morrell Trust who generously funded my research; to my colleagues in the Political Theory Workshop at the University of York, where many of the arguments of the book were first presented and discussed; to Albert Weale and Peter Jones, who provided very helpful and constructive comments on an earlier draft of the manuscript; and to Steven Kennedy, my editor, who has remained good-natured and patient through many extended deadlines. They have all been better friends than I deserve, and I am deeply grateful to them.

A special debt of gratitude is owed to my colleague John Horton, who read and commented on the entire manuscript. Over many years he has been an astute critic and a generous friend. Without his support I would have given up long ago and I wish, for his sake, that this were a better book.

My thanks go the Aristotelian Society for permission to reprint part of my paper 'Liberty and Autonomy', which first appeared in the *Proceedings of the Aristotelian Society*, 1986–7.

Finally, I am grateful to my husband, Andrew, who bought a word processor and did not see it or me for a very long time.

The author's royalties from the sale of this book are donated to Amnesty International.

SUSAN MENDUS

1 The Concept of Toleration

'I hate him for he is a Christian.' (*Merchant of Venice*, Act I, Scene III)

Racial intolerance: preliminary considerations

In modern society, problems of toleration arise most often and most obviously in connection with racial, religious or sexual matters: in Britain, the Brixton disorders of 1981 were held to be both a symptom and a consequence of a deeply embedded racial intolerance. Reporting on the disorders, Lord Scarman remarked; 'All the evidence I have received, both on the subject of racial disadvantage and more generally, suggests that racialism and discrimination against black people – often hidden, sometimes unconscious – remain a major source of social tension and conflict' (Scarman, 1986, p.172). Racial intolerance and discrimination, whilst not identified as the direct cause of disorder, were held to be important social conditions serving to create a disposition towards violent protest of the sort which flared in Brixton on the weekend of 10–12 April 1981. Members of the black community attributed their poverty and deprivation to racial discrimination and, as Scarman puts it; 'once you have deprivation and once minorities perceive that they are at the end of every queue, then race heats up the furnace of anger to an unbearable temperature' (pp.xiv–xv).

If this is the lesson of Brixton, it is a lesson which had been learned long before in America. In the wake of the urban rioting which swept the United States from 1964 onwards, the *Report of the National Advisory Commission on Civil Disorders* (The Kerner Report, 1968) commented upon the attitudes of young blacks

1

involved in the riots. Like the blacks of Brixton, the American
rioters felt strongly that they deserved better jobs, better housing,
better educational opportunities, and that they were prevented
from obtaining these things because of the colour of their skin. In
America, as in Britain, there was deprivation, and black youths
perceived that deprivation as having a racial basis. The Kerner
Report noted;

> 'Characteristically, the typical rioter was not a hoodlum, habitual
> criminal, or riffraff; nor was he a recent migrant, a member of
> an uneducated underclass, or a person lacking broad social and
> political concerns. Instead he was a teenager or young adult, a
> life-long resident of the city in which he rioted, a high-school
> drop-out – but somewhat better educated than his Negro
> neighbor – and almost invariably underemployed or employed
> in a menial job. He was proud of his race, extremely hostile to
> both whites and middle-class Negroes and, although informed
> about politics, highly distrustful of the political system and of
> political leaders.' (Kerner, 1968, p.111)

Thus, in both Britain and America official reports cited deprivation
born of racial discrimination as persistent social factors which
provided at least a partial and indirect explanation of discontent,
disorder and, ultimately, of riot. In Britain, Lord Scarman's
report was enthusiastically received. It was described as 'brilliant',
'forthright', 'one of the great social documents of our time'. But
this general praise did not extend to the Report's references to
racial intolerance and to the problems of multi-racial inner cities.
Far from being applauded, these were greeted with considerable
scepticism. Scarman's call for 'positive action to redress the balance
of racial disadvantage', and his insistence that 'urgent action is
needed if [racial disadvantage] is not to become an endemic,
ineradicable disease threatening the very survival of our society'
were declared irrelevant, potentially harmful to harmonious working relationships, and implicitly unjust. Commenting on this
aspect of the Report, the *Daily Telegraph* claimed 'vague liberal
sentiments are all very well, but not likely to be effective when
things turn nasty' (quoted in Benyon, 1984, p.8). It was this
'typically trendy and liberal viewpoint' about racial matters which
touched a nerve amongst many commentators, who resisted and

resented the implication that Britain was (and is) an intolerant society.

Lacking the American history of discriminatory legislation, of segregation of black and white in separate schools and separate residential areas, and of restrictions on black suffrage, it was urged that in racial matters Britain was a tolerant society. Legislation which went beyond negative tolerance in the direction of affirmative action was thought to be both unfair and counter-productive: unfair because it would give preferential treatment to blacks; counter-productive because it would serve to generate resentment amongst disadvantaged whites. Toleration, it was thought, required only the absence of impediment or discrimination under the law, and in this sense Britain had been a tolerant society for a hundred years or more. But is this sense of toleration enough, or is it true, as Scarman suggests, that more is required?

Sexual toleration and the tyranny of opinion

This book asks three questions: 'What is toleration?', 'What is its justification?' and 'What are its proper limits?' Moreover, it raises these questions as questions central to the liberal tradition in political thought. In the history of political philosophy liberalism has been closely identified with the values of individual liberty and of toleration. Certainly, toleration is not the exclusive preserve of liberals: as we shall see, arguments for toleration pre-date the rise of liberalism, but toleration has a special and privileged status in the liberal tradition. Liberals are frequently *defined* as people who value liberty and the toleration necessary for the promotion of liberty (Arblaster, 1984; Waldron, 1987; Raz, 1982, 1986, 1988; Rawls, 1971). Although other political ideologies may find a place for the value of toleration, it is in liberalism that that place is most exalted. Moreover, it is the liberal tradition which has most robustly defended toleration as a good in itself, not a mere pragmatic device or prudential expedient. But if the values of liberalism are to be more than 'vague sentiments' or 'trendy viewpoints' then we must explain their coherence and seek their justification. We must search for the hard arguments and philosophical insights which underpin liberalism and its commitment to toleration. What, then, are these arguments? How far do they extend, and what do they require of us? Before embarking on attempts to answer those questions, something more must be said about the concept of toleration itself, what it consists in, and how it is to be distinguished from other concepts.

Racial intolerance, whether or not it is an endemic feature of our society, is only one area in which problems of toleration arise. Another area is that of what may broadly be called sexual toleration. Until 1967, when the Sexual Offences Act became law, homosexuality was a criminal offence in Britain, and even now the age of consent for homosexuality is twenty one – five years higher than the age of consent for heterosexual activity. In 1971 the *Gay Liberation Front Manifesto* declared 'reform cannot change the deep down attitude of straight people that homosexuality is at best inferior to their own way of life, at worst a sickening perversion.' And in similar vein, the founding statement of the New York Gay Liberation Front declared; 'We reject society's attempt to impose sexual roles and definitions of our nature. We are stepping out of these roles and simplistic myths. WE ARE GOING TO BE WHO WE ARE.'

Intolerance may take many forms, and what these quotations indicate is that even where there are few legal impediments to homosexuality, social mores may still constitute a very powerful force for intolerance. In his 1859 essay *On Liberty* John Stuart Mill inveighed against what he called 'the tyranny of public opinion', urging that this might constitute a source of intolerance as pervasive and oppressive as any law. Recent events consequent upon the AIDS crisis in Britain and America have done little to falsify Mill's claim, for they bear witness to the fact that intolerance may flourish even in the absence of legal constraint or coercion. Indeed, one of the most crushing forms of intolerance is social disapproval, whether or not backed by legal sanction. There are, therefore, two fronts on which intolerance may manifest itself: the legal front and the social front. Laws may be intolerant or repressive in their restriction of individual diversity, but the attitudes of society may also serve as a signal of intolerance, whatever the legal situation.

In his 1983 Morrell Memorial Address, 'Toleration and the Law', Lord Scarman draws attention to a principle of toleration encapsulated in English law. He says

'Toleration is, and has been for a hundred years or more, part and parcel of the English way of life. But toleration in a legal sense has only a negative content: it is at best a negative virtue. If you were to ask the ordinary man, "What is toleration?" I think he would reply, "Live and let live". Those words are in fact captured in one of the basic mottos of the English common law . . . "So use your own that you do not harm another"' (Scarman, 1987, p.49)

Lord Scarman's contention, together with the examples of racial and sexual intolerance outlined above, raise two distinct but related points about the nature and scope of toleration. Firstly, they emphasise the fact that official legal toleration may not be enough to guarantee toleration overall – toleration requires tolerant attitudes within society as well as tolerant laws. Secondly, they raise the question of what toleration consists in: is it merely a negative matter, a matter of 'living and letting live', or does it require more than that – a positive welcoming of difference? Scarman clearly believes that it requires more. Both in his Report on the Brixton riots, and in his subsequent Address, he emphasises the need to construe toleration in a positive way; 'Man today requires more of the law than that he be left alone to pursue his way of life as he sees fit. Today he asks of the law positive rights enforceable against the state, against his employer, and indeed on occasions against the rest of us' (p.54). Does this mean that he asks for more than toleration, or does it mean that toleration, properly understood, is more than merely letting alone?

These are conceptual questions about the nature of toleration, but they also reflect important features of its history. Lord Scarman notes that historically and legally toleration has been held to consist simply in 'letting alone': it has had negative import only. If the scope of the term is to be extended to include positive duties, some reason must be provided for that: we must investigate the reasons for construing toleration in a more positive way. Such an investigation will concentrate largely (but not exclusively) on the liberal tradition, for it is there that toleration has figured as a central value. Additionally, it will involve reference to the history of toleration, and to an area of the problem not yet mentioned – religious toleration.

Religious toleration: historical and conceptual considerations

It is difficult to exaggerate the importance of religious toleration
in the history of the subject. Indeed, the story of toleration is
predominantly the story of the battle against religious intolerance
and persecution, and it is in this context that many important
conceptual points about the nature and justification of toleration
were first formulated. Moreover, examples of religious intolerance
provide an indication of what the concept of toleration involves
and how it differs from related concepts such as liberty or licence.
I begin, therefore, by discussing some historical examples of
religious intolerance, and by using these to draw attention to the
conditions under which problems of toleration arise. My aim here
is to outline what we may call the circumstances of toleration –
the necessary conditions for the application of the term.

When, in Shakespeare's *The Merchant of Venice*, the Jew
Shylock declares his hatred of the Christian Bassanio, he speaks
against the background of fifteen hundred years of antagonism
between Christian and Jew. Invited to dine with Bassanio, he
replies; 'Yes, to smell pork, to eat of the habitation which your
prophet the Nazarite conjured the devil into! . . . I will not eat
with you, drink with you, nor pray with you' (Act I, Scene III).
Yet on the other side, intolerance of Jews by Christians was even
more virulent: Jews were the original enemies of Christ. They had
procured his crucifixion and thus had his blood upon their hands
and upon the hands of their children. As such, they were a constant
target of persecution and violent hatred, and in sixteenth century
Europe demands increased for the formal segregation of Jews, the
burning of synagogues and the compulsory wearing of distinctive
badges of humiliation. As one historian has put it, in Europe, 'the
sixteenth century became the century of the ghetto' (Bossy, 1985,
p.86).

Moreover, religious intolerance in this period was not confined
to Jews and Christians. In France, the 'Wars of Religion' were
waged between Protestant and Catholic, and were finally quieted
by the Edict of Nantes (1598) which granted to Protestants full
civil rights and the right to worship openly, albeit in specified
regions. The armistice was, however, short-lived. The Catholic
church remained hostile to any degree of toleration of Protestan-
tism, and in 1685 the Edict was revoked. Pastors were given

fourteen days in which to renounce their calling or die. 'I have the right to persecute you because I am right and you are wrong,' declared Bossuet (Bates, 1945, p.164).

In England too religious intolerance was rampant. The Church of England, the Church of Rome, and the Puritan movement were deeply antagonistic one to another, and while each group urged toleration for its own members, few were willing to extend that same toleration to members of other groups. Indeed, in a society which was devoutly and fervently religious, religious toleration was often seen as the greatest heresy of all: in matters of religion, men's immortal souls were at stake, and toleration in this world was not to be granted if the price was damnation in the next. Moreover, and independently of considerations of salvation, the heretic was believed to be committing an offence against God, and for that reason alone was not to be tolerated.

Nevertheless, it is clear that in all these cases toleration was held to consist simply in leaving others alone. Neither the Edict of Nantes nor the Toleration Act did any more than grant to dissenters very limited rights to freedom of worship. The Toleration Act of 1689 provided freedom of worship for all who accepted William and Mary as sovereigns and were also prepared to accept the essentials of the Thirty-nine Articles (the confession of the Church of England). Nevertheless, Catholics and Jews continued long after to suffer many other legal disabilities, and it was not until 1829 and 1846 respectively that these disabilities were finally removed. Lord Scarman's claim that Britain has been tolerant in all matters religious since the middle of the nineteenth century rests upon a concept of toleration which construes it as involving only the absence of legal impediment or obstruction. Historically, to tolerate was to permit by law, but not to endorse or encourage members of dissenting groups, much less to provide them with equal opportunities.

A further point which these historical examples indicate is the close emotional connection between intolerance and a commitment to truth: Bossuet's justification of his own intolerant attitude rests on the assumption that intolerance is permitted – even required – in circumstances where there is a right way to behave. His attitude is not dissimilar to those who would nowadays repress homosexuality as a perversion: like Bossuet, their justification of intolerance is that there is a correct way to live, and that nothing can be gained by allowing people to live in a manner which is deeply misguided and morally wrong.

The circumstances of toleration

These examples of religious, racial and sexual intolerance, give rise to the three questions which will form the central concern of this book. They also suggest answers to those questions. They suggest that toleration is simply a matter of leaving others alone or refraining from persecuting them. They appear to imply (though, as we shall see later, appearances may be deceptive) that it is limited by considerations of truth, and justified by reference to scepticism. First and foremost, however, they give some indication of the circumstances in which questions of toleration arise. They point to the necessary conditions for toleration and indicate the differences between it and related concepts.

There are two features common to all the cases so far described: the first is that the problem of toleration arises in circumstances of diversity. The second is that toleration is required where the nature of the diversity is such as to give rise to disapproval, dislike, or disgust. Thus Shylock's intolerance of Bassanio is grounded both in the fact that Jews and Christians adopted different practices, and in the feelings of disgust generated by those practices (for example, the eating of pork). Similarly, intolerance of homosexuals is grounded both in the fact of their different sexual practices, and in the belief that those practices are 'at best inferior' to heterosexuality and 'at worst a sickening perversion'. These features (diversity coupled with disapproval, dislike or disgust) may be called the *circumstances* of toleration, since they isolate the conditions under which we may properly speak of toleration as opposed to liberty, licence or indifference. Simply to allow the different practices of others, whilst not objecting to them, disapproving of them, or finding them repugnant, is not to display tolerance, but only to favour liberty. As one writer has recently put it;

'Toleration is a disagreeable subject. This is because the question of toleration arises only in connection with disagreeable things: heresy, subversion, prostitution, drug-abuse, pornography, abortion and cruelty to animals. It can hardly be edifying for the mind to dwell on such subjects. But if there were not things we disapproved of, the concept of 'toleration' need not be introduced at all. It would be enough to talk about 'liberty' or 'freedom'. When we speak of people's liberty or freedom, no criticism is implied of the use to which they put their freedom . . . but only the undesirable – or at any rate, the undesired, is a candidate for toleration.' (Cranston, 1987, p.101)

A further necessary condition of toleration is that the tolerator must be in a position to influence the behaviour of the tolerated: thus, in the religious examples, we may be said to tolerate only in circumstances where, although we disapprove of the heterodox religion, and although we have the power to persecute, we nevertheless refrain. This power may or may not be a legal power: even though, as individuals, we are not in a position to alter the laws governing homosexuality, we may still display intolerance towards homosexuals by bringing social pressure to bear upon them. Mill's 'tyranny of public opinion' is as much a manifestation of intolerance as was the Sexual Offences Act prior to 1967.

These, then, are the circumstances in which questions of toleration arise – circumstances of diversity coupled with dislike, disapproval, or disgust. And it is, further, a necessary condition of toleration that the tolerator should have the power to interfere with, influence, or remove the offending practice, but refrain from using that power. In stating this last necessary condition of toleration, I am of course glossing over the crucial question, raised earlier, of whether toleration requires *more* than mere refusal to interfere – *more* than merely 'leaving alone'. Additionally, I am ignoring the many controversies which surround the interpretation of 'leaving alone' – itself a problematic concept. All I am suggesting is that such a refusal is at least a *necessary* condition of toleration. Whether it is also a *sufficient* condition will be considered later.

The scope of toleration

In setting out the circumstances of toleration, reference has been made indifferently to dislike, disapproval and disgust. It has been implicitly assumed that any or all of these may serve to define

cases in which questions of toleration arise. However, there are
important differences between the concepts. In particular, there
are important differences between morally grounded disapproval
and simple dislike, distaste or disgust. The differences are such as
to lead some to urge that talk of toleration is appropriate in the
first case only. Thus, Peter Nicholson writes:

> 'we must see the moral idea of toleration solely in terms of
> disapproval, i.e. of the making of judgements and the holding
> of reasons over which argument is possible. Toleration is a
> matter of moral choice, and our tastes and inclinations are
> irrelevant. No doubt, people's prejudices, their contingent
> feelings of liking or disliking, have to be taken into account
> when one is trying to explain why they are tolerant or not; but
> such feelings are not morally grounded, and cannot be the
> ground of a moral position.' (Nicholson, 1985, pp.160–1)

By contrast, Mary Warnock insists that toleration has a wider
scope and may be displayed in cases where there is a simple dislike
as well as in cases where there is moral disapproval. She remarks:

> 'Often one would think oneself tolerant if one refrained from
> criticising something that one disliked, hated, or regarded with
> varying degrees of distaste. . . . More fundamentally, I simply
> do not believe that a distinction can be drawn, as Nicholson
> seeks to draw it, between the moral and the non-moral, resting
> on the presumption that the moral is rational, or subject to
> argument, the non-moral a matter of feeling or sentiment.'
> (Warnock, 1987, pp.25–6)

The debate as to whether the scope of toleration is such as to
cover both things of which we disapprove and things which we
dislike is not merely a verbal dispute. It is part of a general
philosophical debate about the very status of moral judgements,
and the nature of the distinction between such judgements and
judgements of taste or preference. Nicholson's claim that toleration
arises only where there is moral disapproval rests on the belief
that a clear distinction may be drawn between the moral, which is
amenable to rational argument, and the non-moral, which is a
matter of bare emotion, feeling, or sentiment, and as such not

amenable to rational argument. However, Mary Warnock insists that such a distinction cannot be sustained. In her opinion, part of the answer to the question 'Ought this to be tolerated?' may come from the strong feelings aroused by the thing in question. 'The intolerable' she says 'is the unbearable. And we may simply feel, believe, conclude without reason, that something is unbearable and must be stopped' (p.126). On her view, there is no clear and decisive distinction between moral judgements which are based on reason, and non-moral judgements which are based on feeling: on the contrary, moral judgements may themselves be based on strong feeling. Following the eighteenth-century philosopher, David Hume, she claims that morality is more properly felt than judged of, and that moral distinctions are not grounded in reason. If she and Hume are correct, then there is no justification for restricting the application of the term 'toleration' to cases where moral disapproval is involved. We ordinarily speak of tolerating in cases where there is only dislike as well as in cases where there is disapproval and, on Warnock's account, this ordinary way of talking reflects a general philosophical truth – that moral judgements are not separated from judgements of taste by an unbridgeable divide.

It is important to be clear about exactly what Warnock is claiming here: in defending the wider scope of toleration she says, 'I am tolerant if one of my daughter's boy friends wears sandals with his suit . . . and I not only make no mention of this outrage, but actually express myself pleased when they declare their intention of getting married' (p.125). The example is, deliberately, a trivial one: it involves no appeal to moral judgement, but only to judgements of taste or preference, and to trivial preferences at that. It refers to the bare emotions which we may feel when confronted with something we dislike or find aesthetically displeasing. However, in suggesting that moral judgements themselves may be based on feeling, Warnock is not assimilating all cases of toleration to this trivial case. From the fact that (some) moral judgements are based on feelings, and that (some) feelings are trivial, it does not follow that all moral judgements are trivial.

Warnock is not claiming that 'there is no difference between torturing a child and wearing sandals with a suit'. 'All I maintain' she says 'is that no sharp line can be drawn between what I dislike and what I disapprove of' (p.127). But of course it does not follow from this that no line can be drawn at all. Quite the reverse, for she goes on to indicate her belief that a line can be drawn when she suggests that the toleration which involves moral disapproval should be termed 'strong toleration', whereas the toleration which involves only dislike should be termed 'weak toleration'. The only proviso being that the distinction between strong and weak toleration, like the distinction between disapproval and dislike, is not invariably clear and uncontroversial.

A further point which should be noted about Warnock's argument, and which will be important later, is that it is concerned with the possible *grounds* of moral judgements, not with their *force*. The question 'Why do we make the moral judgements we do make?' is distinct and separable from the question, 'What are we committed to in making a moral judgement?' It is the former, not the latter question which Warnock is addressing. She is concerned with the factors which prompt us to say that something is morally wrong, not with the implications of our saying that that thing is wrong. Here, anyway, is one argument which purports to show that toleration has a wide scope – that it extends over more than the moral realm.

A second, related reason for favouring this wider scope is provided by what is sometimes known as value pluralism. Like most philosophical theories, pluralism comes in many forms. However, in broad and general terms, pluralists construe the moral world as consisting of distinct, and often mutually incompatible (even incommensurable) values or sets of values. They believe that a world in which all value conflict has been eliminated would be a poorer world than one in which value conflict exists. The reason for this is that pluralism dictates that the elimination of conflict often involves the elimination of things which are valuable. According to this theory there is no one set of virtues which is exhaustive, nor one set of values which is all-embracing.

The most famous exponent of value pluralism in political philosophy is Sir Isaiah Berlin. In his seminal essay 'Two Concepts of Liberty' he says:

'One belief, more than any other, is responsible for the slaughter of individuals on the altars of the great historical ideals . . . this is the belief that somewhere, in the past or in the future, in divine revelation or in the mind of an individual thinker, in the pronouncements of history or science, or in the simple heart of an uncorrupted good man, there is a final solution. This ancient faith rests on the conviction that all the positive values in which men have believed must, in the end, be compatible and perhaps even entail one another.' (Berlin, 1969, p.167)

What is remarkable about this passage is the explicit connection it makes between the denial of pluralism and the flourishing of intolerance. The belief that all values can be reconciled, the belief that there is a single right answer to moral and political problems, generates tyranny and oppression. On the other hand, pluralism requires toleration because it insists that not all values can be reconciled harmoniously. On a political level, this means that there is no single, utopian state in which all conflict is eliminated and no value is lost: for example, the requirements of liberty and of equality will conflict, as will the demands of justice and of mercy. To pursue perfect justice will, of necessity, be to renounce mercy, and vice versa.

Most importantly for our purposes, a commitment to pluralism also serves to clarify the point of construing toleration widely, so as to include both things of which we disapprove morally and things which we dislike. It provides a further justification of Warnock's contention that 'toleration' may be used in both a strong and a weak sense. To see why this is so, we need to look at toleration on an individual as well as on a political level, for the belief that not all values can be reconciled applies here too. Thus, pluralism dictates that no one person can possess all virtues and all good qualities: some virtues are such that the possession of them entails the absence of other, equally valuable, yet incompatible virtues. Furthermore, whilst we cannot speak of tolerating other people's virtues, we can speak of tolerating their limitations, and we may do so whilst recognising that these limitations are necessary concomitants of those virtues. As Joseph Raz has put it;

'The reason people lack certain virtues or accomplishments may be, and often is, that they possess other and incompatible virtues and accomplishments. When we tolerate the limitations of others we may be aware that these are but the other side of their personal virtues and strengths. This may indeed be the reason

> why we tolerate them . . . The fact that intolerance can be directed at people's limitations and that those can be aspects of some other virtues which those people possess acquires special significance for those who believe in value pluralism. It provides the link between pluralism and toleration.' (Raz, 1986, pp.402–3)

An example of this, at the individual level, is the virtue of judiciousness: we may value a person for his sound judgement, his careful analysis of problems and dilemmas, and his thoughtful responses to difficult situations. In some circumstances, however, such a virtue may present itself as a defect: proper thoughtfulness in one context, may be infuriating indecision in another, and sometimes we need people who will act, not people who will carefully weigh up all sides of the problem. Thus, we may tolerate people's limitations, and tolerate them precisely because we see that those limitations are but the reverse side of their virtues, without which the virtues themselves would not exist. The claim that toleration may extend to limitations as well as to vices, is thus unsurprising for the pluralist.

Of course, this view of the scope of toleration depends upon a value pluralism according to which it is indeed impossible that people should simultaneously possess all desirable qualities, accomplishments or virtues. If, with Plato, we assume the opposite – if, that is to say, we assume that all virtues can be reconciled, then this particular ground for toleration disappears. Most importantly, the reason for extending the scope of toleration to include limitations, or weaknesses, as well as moral vices, disappears. These two grounds for favouring a wider rather than a narrower scope for toleration (for accommodating both toleration in a strong sense and toleration in a weak sense) are connected one to another in so far as they both depend upon the denial of a particular form of moral objectivity. Both Warnock and Raz, in their different ways, deny central features of a Platonic theory of morality, according to which moral truth is rationally discoverable and internally consistent. In other words, they both deny the assimilation of moral truth to factual truth, urging in the first case that moral judgements are not necessarily founded on reason, but are felt; in the second case, that moral values are not all compatible one with another. They appear, moreover, to be supporting the belief that there is an emotional kinship between toleration and scepticism – or at least to be suggesting that some defences of toleration are most naturally allied to a denial of strong ethical rationalism. These claims about the nature and status of moral judgements will be of considerable importance when we come to consider the justifications of toleration offered by Locke and Mill. For the moment, however, it is enough to note simply that both the scope and the justification of toleration may be influenced by theories about the status of moral judgements.

These opening sections have raised, in very general terms, the question 'What is toleration?' It has been noted that toleration is distinct from both liberty and licence in that questions of toleration arise only where there is diversity coupled with disapproval, dislike or disgust. These are the circumstances of toleration. References to disapproval and dislike, however, raise questions about the scope of toleration, and here there are two schools of thought: some believe that toleration is a concept which can properly be applied only to things of which we disapprove morally. Others claim that it may equally properly be applied to things which are merely disliked. The former construe toleration narrowly, the latter more widely.

In discussing the relative merits of the two schools of thought, the latter was favoured, partly because it conforms better to ordinary usage. However, this wider interpretation of toleration poses problems for our understanding of racial toleration. Those who favour a narrow, morally-based account of toleration must presumably deny the propriety of speaking of racial intolerance, since it is odd to link racial discrimination, or intolerance, to moral disapproval. Most frequently the racist is motivated by dislike or disgust. Prejudice and bigotry, not moral disapproval, are the hallmarks of racism. Does this simply reinforce the belief that toleration is to be construed widely rather than narrowly? We do, after all, commonly speak of toleration in connection with race, and it might appear that any account of the concept of toleration which rules out such a use is, prima facie, defective. However, when we move from questions about the circumstances and scope of toleration to questions about what it requires of us and what its proper objects are, the arguments may lead in a different direction.

In discussing the requirements of toleration, two opposing positions were referred to: the claim that toleration requires only that we leave others alone or refrain from persecuting them (the negative interpretation of toleration), and the claim, supported by Lord Scarman, that toleration requires more than that – that it requires assisting, aiding and fostering (the positive interpretation of toleration). The demand that toleration be construed positively sits well with situations in which the objects of toleration are things which are not morally wrong and which are unalterable. Such is the case with racial discrimination. Skin colour, or racial origin, are not proper objects of moral disapproval, nor are they features over which individuals have any control.

The two points are, perhaps, connected. Moral philosophers often claim that 'ought' implies 'can'. Moral approval and disapproval are legitimate only on the assumption that the agent can in fact change the thing disapproved of, or has some control over the thing approved of. Where something is unalterable, no praise or blame may properly accrue. In such circumstances tolerating may well involve compensating for the ungrounded and irrational dislike of others. It may involve positive action. But what is implied in this demand is that the persecution or discrimination is itself illegitimate, since aimed at something unalterable. And this in turn suggests that only those things which can be changed are legitimate objects of toleration. It suggests that actions may be proper objects of toleration, since they are things over which the agent has a certain amount of control. Beliefs, however, are rather more resistant to alteration. And skin colour or racial origin are wholly outside the control of the individual.

The foregoing argument suggests that talk of toleration in the racial context is misleading, for to speak of toleration implies that the thing tolerated can be changed – that it is something alterable, and that it is to the agent's discredit that he or she does not alter it. It implies that there really is something wrong with belonging to another race, or being of a different colour, and thus lends some spurious credibility to the claims of racists. Mary Warnock's objection to her son-in-law's sandals certainly carries no moral implication, but it does carry an implication of alterability and of discredit. It is proper to say that she tolerates him at least partly because it is proper to say that his behaviour is something over which he has some control. To treat race analogously is, however, potentially misleading, for it implies that blacks or Asians are similarly tolerated and therefore are similarly at fault in not modifying the feature which is offensive to others. Yet more worryingly, it implies that the dislike and disgust of the racist are in some sense legitimate. All this may lead us to wonder whether 'toleration' is an appropriate term to use in the case of racial discrimination and disadvantage.

The racial and sexual examples thus generate questions about the proper objects of toleration: is it correct to speak of tolerating people as such, or can we properly be said only to tolerate beliefs, or practices, or behaviour? Racial intolerance seems to be directed at the person quite independent of any beliefs or opinions which the person may hold. Indeed, in this case intolerance is directed at a feature of the person which is unalterable. Even if we accept the wider scope of the term 'toleration' and take it to cover both things which are disliked and things which are disapproved of, we may nevertheless wonder whether intolerance can be rational when applied to unalterable facets of life, to things over which the agent has no control.

Consideration of ordinary usage thus suggests that the concept of toleration is wide, covering both things disliked and things disapproved of. On the other hand, consideration of the objects of toleration suggests that we may legitimately be said to tolerate only those things which are, in principle, alterable, and that, in a slightly different way, may lead us to favour a narrower employment of the term.

The preceding discussions highlight the problematic nature of the concept of toleration: the circumstances in which the concept applies may be clear (circumstances of diversity coupled with dislike, disapproval or disgust), but to say any more than this is to enter into areas of profound controversy. The *scope* of toleration is unclear: should we restrict the term to cases where moral disapproval is implied, or should we range wider than that? Similarly, we may ask what are the *requirements* of toleration. Does it require forebearance only, or is there an obligation to protect and preserve? Does toleration require more than merely letting alone? Does it require assisting and nurturing? Finally, it is a matter of dispute what the proper *objects* of toleration are: can we properly include only that which is alterable, or is it legitimate to speak of tolerating a person in respect of something over which he has no control? May we speak of tolerating people themselves, or must we tolerate (or be intolerant of) practices,

attitudes, and beliefs? Different responses to these questions will
be discussed in the following chapters, but I shall turn now to a
central problem of toleration – its paradoxical nature. The paradox
arises when toleration has a moral grounding, and where the
practice which is tolerated is alterable or (to some extent) within
the control of the agent.

The paradox of toleration

Many of the truly difficult cases in which the question of toleration
arises are cases in which the tolerator disapproves morally of the
thing tolerated. Whatever may be said about the possibility of
tolerating people's limitations, and whatever points may be made
about the grounding of toleration in strong feeling as well as in
rational judgement, it is nevertheless true that amongst the most
problematic cases of toleration are those in which what is tolerated
is believed to be morally wrong (not merely disliked) and where
it is held that there are no compensating virtues associated with
the thing tolerated. Religious examples are amongst the most
obvious here: Bossuet's claim, 'I have the right to persecute you
because I am right and you are wrong' exemplifies precisely the
difficulty: where people believe that what they are being asked to
tolerate is wrong, and where they further believe that nothing
would be lost if that practice did not exist, it is hard to explain
why, nevertheless, the thing should be tolerated.

The point applies equally to the religious case and to the case
of homosexuality, mentioned above. Those who genuinely believe
that homosexuality is morally wrong – that it is a perversion – may
also believe that nothing of value would be lost if it were legally
forbidden and if those who engage in it were (for their own good)
criminally punished. Of course, we need not think this way about
different religious or sexual practices. But if we do, it becomes
increasingly difficult to explain why we should tolerate them. This
point, moreover, is not merely a psychological one about the
difficulty of persuading people of strong conviction of the propriety
of tolerating that of which they disapprove deeply. It is a conceptual
point which presents in stark form what may be called the pardox
of toleration.

The paradox is this: normally, we count toleration as a virtue in individuals and a duty in societies. However, where toleration is based on moral disapproval, it implies that the thing tolerated is wrong and ought not to exist. The question which then arises is why, given the claim to objectivity incorporated in the strong sense of toleration, it should be thought good to tolerate. By contrast, cases in which toleration is based merely on dislike do not raise the same problem of objectivity, for my dislike of something is distinct from my belief that that thing is morally wrong in just this sense, that there is not necessarily a commitment to the idea that the world would be a better place if the thing did not exist. And the same, of course, is true of limitations. Indeed, in the case of limitations, it might well be that the very reason for tolerating them is the recognition that the world would – all things considered – be worse without them since if they went, the corresponding virtues would also go. However, in the religious examples considered, and in most of the truly problematic cases of toleration, the situation is not so simple. In the example of religious intolerance given at the head of this chapter, there is no belief on the part of Christians that the world would be a worse place if Jewish belief and practice did not exist. Nor vice-versa. So even if we allow that toleration may be extended so as to include both things which are disliked and things which are thought morally wrong, both limitations and vices, the fact remains that the most problematic cases are cases of the latter sort. Cases where we must tolerate in a strong sense. Moreover, there is, in this fact, a notorious puzzle, which is elegantly expressed by D. D. Raphael in a recent paper called 'The Intolerable'. Raphael says;

'to disapprove of something is to judge it to be wrong. Such a judgement does not express a purely subjective preference. It claims universality; it claims to be the view of any rational agent. The content of the judgement, that something is wrong, implies that the something may properly be prevented. But if your disapproval is reasonably grounded, why should you go against it at all? Why should you tolerate?' (Raphael, 1988, p.139)

It might appear that this line of argument contradicts the argument presented by Mary Warnock and outlined above. Where Warnock claims that no clear line can be drawn between moral and non-moral judgements, Raphael insists that there are very definite differences between the two: moral judgements claim objectivity, whereas non-moral judgements express purely subjective prefer- ences. However, there is not necessarily a contradiction between the two. Warnock's argument is an argument about the *grounding* of moral as against non-moral judgements, and her claim is the Humean claim that moral judgements are not (or not necessarily) grounded in reason. Raphael, on the other hand, is presenting an argument about the *logical implications* of moral judgements, and his claim is that when I make a moral judgement (however it is grounded) I am claiming universal validity. The distinction is thus a distinction between what prompts me to say that something is morally wrong (that I don't want it to exist) and what I mean by saying that something is morally wrong (it ought not to exist). As we have seen, these two questions, though related, are distinct and separable. The paradox of toleration arises because, however they are grounded, people's moral judgements claim universal validity – they claim to be the view of any rational agent.

In this book, emphasis will be placed upon the attempt to find a solution to this paradox. However, it is worth mentioning here that some of the superficially simpler cases (the cases involving toleration in the weak sense) may themselves provide a route to the solution of more problematic ones. In other words, value pluralism, and the role of feelings in morality, may offer a method of understanding the justification, grounds and limits of toleration quite generally.

The situation which confronts us, therefore, is this: the circum- stances of toleration are circumstances in which there is diversity coupled with disapproval, dislike, or disgust, and where the tolerator has the power to influence the tolerated. In cases where toleration involves more than mere dislike, and has moral force, a paradox arises, which involves explaining how the tolerator might think it good to tolerate that which is morally wrong. In other words, we need to show how we can consistently claim *both* that toleration is a virtue in individuals and a good in society, *and* that (strong) toleration necessarily and conceptually involves reference to things believed to be morally disreputable, or evil.

In an attempt to solve this problem, my strategy will be as follows: firstly, I shall look at two texts which have set the agenda for the philosophical discussion of toleration. These are John Locke's *Epistola de Tolerantia* (*Letter on Toleration*) and John

Stuart Mill's seminal essay *On Liberty*. Each of these texts operates on two levels: firstly, each is written in response to a particular practical problem of toleration (in Locke's case, the problem of religious toleration in seventeenth century Britain; in Mill's case, the problem of the 'tyranny of public opinion' in Victorian Britain). Secondly, however, and most importantly for our purposes, each provides a general philosophical justification of toleration. The next two chapters, therefore, will serve the dual purpose of describing, in general terms, the historical development of the problem of toleration, and of examining critically two different kinds of philosophical justification of it.

Building upon the theories of Locke and Mill, the two subsequent chapters will discuss the grounds and the limits of toleration. What are the reasons for thinking it good, and what are its limits? Finally, the arguments presented and discussed in earlier chapters will be drawn together to indicate the importance of the concept, and the relationship between it and associated concepts in political thought, such as those of liberty and of equality. A theory of toleration will be presented which will be such as to exhibit its grounds and nature both as an individual virtue and as a political right. I begin, however, with two texts central to the problem of toleration – John Locke's *Epistola de Tolerantia*, and John Stuart Mill's *On Liberty*.

2 Locke and the Case for Rationality

'I shall not try to write the history of intolerance: that would be to write the history of the world.' (Bates, p.132)

The struggle for toleration begins philosophically with Plato's demand in *Republic* that (at least some) artists be banished from the ideal state. Historically, it may even be said to begin in the Garden of Eden, when the curse of intolerance is Adam's punishment for sin ('I will put enmity between thee and the woman, and between thy seed and her seed'. Genesis, 3.15). For my purposes, however, the history begins in the seventeenth century, the period which saw the publication of John Locke's seminal text, *Epistola de Tolerantia*. The importance of Locke's work lies both in its response to the specific practical problems of religious toleration in the Reformation period in Britain and Europe, and in its attempt to provide a more general philosophical justification of toleration, particularly of the toleration of religious diversity. Most importantly, however, Locke's political philosophy signals the birth of liberalism, and his *Letter on Toleration* constitutes an early attempt to provide a liberal justification of toleration.

In this chapter, I shall look at the historical provenance and philosophical significance of Locke's *Letter*. My aim will be to suggest that, contrary to the opinions of many modern commentators, there is something philosophically important in his account and something which is worth retaining and carrying over into modern analyses of the problem. I begin, however, by giving a brief outline of the historical circumstances which surrounded the writing of the *Letter*.

The historical background

As has already been mentioned, the seventeenth century was a period of enormous religious antagonism both in Britain and Europe generally. In France, the Edict of Nantes (1598), which granted a degree of religious toleration to dissenters, was short lived and by 1685 had been revoked, thus signalling a return to religious intolerance. In Britain, the situation was yet more complicated: Henry VIII's break with Rome, motivated more by personal than religious considerations, paved the way for a period of strife and uncertainty during which the English throne was occupied by sovereigns of varying religious beliefs and differing degrees of enthusiasm in imposing those beliefs upon the population at large.

Moreover, religious strife was not confined to Anglicans and Catholics: the rise of Puritanism in Britain, and the authoritarian and arbitrary acts of the Stuart kings eventually culminated in Civil War. Yet even here, the broadly tolerant policies of Cromwell were not to outlive his death. The revolution of 1642–9, which led to the death of the king and the declaration of a republic, was hotly followed in 1688 by a further, if less bloody, revolution. In the intervening period dissenters, including Locke himself, had been forced to flee England. If the sixteenth century was the century of the ghetto, the seventeenth century was assuredly the century of revolution. It was the century in which long-held grievances associated with religious and political persecution finally erupted in civil strife.

It is against this background of uncertain religious toleration and prolonged civil unrest that Locke's *Letter* must be read. His own involvement in the events leading up to the revolution of 1688, his close association with the Earl of Shaftesbury (a leading political figure in opposition to the king), and his profound religious commitment to Puritanism, all inform and shape the work. Indeed, some commentators have gone so far as to suggest that the *Letter* is so deeply imbued with the spirit of its age as to be of little or no philosophical interest to us today. Thus one commentator writes:

'For twentieth century liberals the problem of toleration is one that concerns the full liberty of belief and behaviour compatible with the necessary authority of a civil magistrate or power. How much does Locke contribute to our understanding of that problem? Locke says little, if anything, that is directly applicable . . . the essential role played by God in Locke's argument about liberty of conscience and toleration precludes any real contribution to contemporary debates about toleration.' (Kelly, 1984)

And again

'Locke's argument requires us to distinguish sharply between the grounds which he offers for his conclusions and the content of those conclusions themselves. And once we draw this rather obvious distinction it then underlines the yawning chasm between the implications of Locke's argument for tolerating varieties of Christian belief and practice within a Christian state and society and the implications which they would bear for freedom of thought and expression more broadly within a secular state or a more intractably plural religious culture.' (John Dunn, 'What is Living and What is Dead in the Philosophy of John Locke', unpublished paper)

The import of these quotations is to suggest that Locke's case for toleration is well and truly dead. However, where the former quotation emphasises Locke's own belief in God and the way in which the belief figures as an essential premise in his case against religious intolerance, the latter quotation emphasises the Christian belief of Locke's audience and the way in which that assumption restricts the scope of his case against religious intolerance. In other words, the first quotation dwells upon the kinds of arguments which philosophers may properly employ; the second argument dwells upon the kinds of people philosophers may properly hope to convince. On the first analysis, Locke's account is based upon a false premise and is therefore invalid. On the second analysis, Locke's account is addressed only to Christian believers, and is therefore incomplete. Either way, his case against religious intolerance is profoundly inadequate once the truth of Christianity is questioned – as it frequently is in modern society. How much importance should we place on these criticisms of Locke's *Letter*?

It is undeniable that the *Letter on Toleration* is, in part, the product of its time. It was written in and for a world where the *fact* of religious belief was rarely questioned and where varieties of religious belief were most often assumed to be varieties of Christianity. Locke refers fleetingly to the toleration of Muslims and 'infidels', but in the final analysis the arguments of the *Letter* 'depend upon accepting the truth of the Christian religion (or at least of some monotheistic religion in which authentic belief is a precondition for valid religious worship and religious worship is the central duty for man)' (Dunn, 1984, p.57). Moreover, in the *Letter* Locke does not hesitate to display his own profound Puritan conviction that 'the care of each man's salvation belongs only to himself'. This, as we shall see, was a belief which incorporated philosophical principle, but also evinced historically specific attitudes to Catholicism and atheism. As one commentator has put it;

> 'The *Letter on Toleration* is an interesting document because, as a contribution to the political debate on toleration, it represents an attempt both to occupy the higher ground of principles and at the same time to rake up the most basic antipopery prejudices and fears that shaped the popular response to James's policies.' (Ashcraft, 1986, p.498)

In understanding and interpreting the work, it is certainly necessary to see it in its historical context, and to consider it as a response to the specific historical events of seventeenth-century Britain and Europe. At the same time, however, the *Letter* is a philosophical text: it purports to provide a quite general justification of religious toleration, and also to describe its proper limits. 'Let us inquire how far the Duty of Toleration extends, and what is required from every one by it,' Locke writes. Thus, although the *Letter* is confined to specifically religious toleration, and although, even there, it concentrates on the 'mutual toleration of *Christians* in their different Professions of Religion', we might nevertheless expect that consideration of these questions would also have implications for questions of toleration more generally. To see whether this expectation is realised, I shall begin by examining the central form of Locke's argument.

Crudely put, the *Letter on Toleration* presents the following case for religious toleration in respect of Christians: the state is defined in terms of the means at its disposal. These are 'to give orders by decree and compel with the sword': 'rods and axes', 'force and blood', 'fire and the sword' are the means characteristically available to the magistrate. Yet, according to Locke, these means are not simply inefficient, but in principle incapable of inducing genuine religious belief. They operate on the will, but belief is not subject to the will, and so those who would attempt to induce religious belief by applying the coercive means at the disposal of the state are engaged in fundamental irrationality. They are attempting to deploy a set of means inappropriate to the end which they desire to obtain.

In order fully to understand Locke's case against religious intolerance it is essential to bear in mind the following points: first, that this is indeed a case for specifically religious toleration. Of course, the claim that belief is not subject to the will is, if true at all, then true quite generally. However, its importance here is that religious belief is concerned with salvation, and salvation is to be attained only by genuine belief, not by insincere profession of faith. Locke's claim therefore is that the civil magistrate who resorts to intolerance or persecution will achieve no more than outward conformity. People can be threatened and coerced into *professions* of belief; they cannot be coerced into *genuine* belief. And genuine belief (inward commitment) is what is required for salvation. It is thus the irrationality of specifically religious intolerance which Locke appeals to to justify his case. So far, the criticisms mentioned above appear wholly in order: we have here a very restricted argument for toleration, which tells us nothing about its justification in cases other than the religious one.

The second point to bear in mind is that Locke's argument is an argument against certain *reasons* for religious intolerance. As we have seen, what is irrational is the attempt to induce religious belief by coercive means. There is, however, nothing intrinsically irrational in religious intolerance engaged in for other purposes – to keep civil peace, for example. Locke's case is thus a minimalist and pragmatic case against persecution. It is not a positive case for diversity of religious belief: Locke thinks it irrational to attempt to coerce people into holding the correct religious belief, but he does not think it always inappropriate to outlaw certain religious practices if, for example, they constitute a danger to the state. His own example is instructive here:

'But if peradventure such were the state of things, that the Interest of the Commonwealth required all slaughter of Beasts should be forborn for some while, in order to the increasing of the stock of Cattel, that had been destroyed by some extraordinary Murain; Who sees not that the Magistrate, in such a case, may forbid all his Subjects to kill any Calves for any use whatsoever? Only 'tis to be observed, that in this case, the Law is not made about a Religious, but a Political matter: nor is the Sacrifice, but the Slaughter of Calves thereby prohibited.' (Tully, 1983, p.42)

This distinction between the reasons for intolerance and the consequences of intolerance highlights an important difference between Locke's case and the case made by Mill and many modern liberals. In Mill's *On Liberty* much is made of the importance of diversity and of the need to foster a society which contains a rich diversity of styles of life. Indeed, Mill sometimes advocates such diversity as a good in itself. In common with some modern liberals he places emphasis on the consequences of intolerance, namely that it will generate dull uniformity. By contrast, Locke has no such commitment to the value of diversity and does not subscribe to the idea of a good society as one which can accommodate a wide variety of different beliefs. The focus of attention is therefore quite different from that which we appear to find in Mill and in modern liberals generally. In later chapters I shall question this modern liberal commitment to diversity, and suggest that many liberals (including Mill) are not in fact as committed to plurality and diversity as they purport to be. For now, however, it is enough to note that there is at least a superficial difference between Locke and modern liberals in this respect: Locke never advocates diversity as a good in itself, whereas for Mill diversity is of central importance.

The third and final point to bear in mind is that Locke's argument against religious intolerance is addressed to the would-be perpetrators of intolerance, not to their victims. It aims to persuade the magistrate of the irrationality of suppression or persecution, but it says little about the wrong done to victims of intolerance. Again, this points a contrast between Locke's defence and most modern defences of toleration. Locke emphasises the irrationality of would-be persecutors, whereas modern liberals concentrate on the wrong done to the persecuted.

In each of these respects Locke's account has been said to be deficient and at odds with modern ways of viewing the problem: where we might ask what is the morality of intolerance, Locke asks whether it is rational. Where we might ask what are the consequences of intolerance, Locke asks what motivates it. And where we might focus on the rights of the tolerated, Locke focuses on the rationality of the tolerators. These three areas – morality and rationality; consequences and reasons; tolerated and tolerators – are the three areas where, it is often suggested, Locke concentrates on wholly the wrong aspect of the problem. Whether or not it is true that Locke's emphasis is misplaced, these three areas will serve to draw attention to the variety of ways in which toleration may be justified, and to the inherent limitations and virtues of different ways of looking at the problem.

Morality and rationality

I begin with Locke's claim that intolerance is to be eschewed because it is (in the religious case) fundamentally irrational. The objection which is standardly made against this argument is that the emphasis on irrationality is wholly misplaced, and can be seen to be so from a modern perspective. We need to understand and explain why intolerance in general is morally wrong. All Locke tells us is why it is irrational in the specific case of religious belief. Therefore, the argument goes, Locke fails on two counts: he confines himself to the religious case and thus renders his argument too narrow for a secular society. Additionally, he imagines that by showing why intolerance is irrational 'he is excused from the messy business of indicating the reasons why it is wrong' (Waldron, 1988, p.86). Both these arguments, in their different ways, focus on the alleged historical specificity of Locke's account. They imply that his argument was a response to the particular practical problems of seventeenth-century Britain, but do not constitute a philosophically compelling case against intolerance in general. In this section I shall discuss Locke's claim that intolerance is irrational and suggest that, *pace* the modern commentators mentioned earlier, it does contain philosophically important features which are relevant to modern concerns.

At the outset, however, it is important to discuss one objection to Locke's account which concentrates not on its historical specificity, nor on its narrowness, but on its validity. As has been mentioned already, Locke's argument centres around the alleged impossibility of deploying the coercive means available to the state in order to bring about conformity of belief in general, and of religious belief in particular. 'It is only Light and Evidence that can work a change in Mens Opinions' he says and 'Light can in no manner proceed from corporal Sufferings, or any other outward Penalties' (p.27). The points here are these: firstly, that belief is necessary for salvation; and secondly that belief cannot be induced by external threat and punishment. Religious intolerance may compel outward conformity, but it cannot compel the genuine belief which is necessary for salvation. Again the Puritan influence is evident: religious toleration is required because believing in God is something one can only do for oneself. Imposed conformity is therefore pointless, since incapable of generating authentic belief. Commenting on this argument, Jeremy Waldron perceives in it a fatal flaw which, he claims, serves to undermine Locke's case. The flaw appears when we consider not the state of belief itself and its immunity from interference, but rather the 'epistemic apparatus' that surrounds and supports belief. Waldron remarks;

'Suppose the religious authorities know that there are certain books that would be sufficient, if read, to shake the faith of an otherwise orthodox population. Then, although again people's beliefs cannot be controlled directly by coercive means, those who wield political power can put it to work indirectly to reinforce belief by banning everyone on pain of death from reading or obtaining copies of these heretical tomes. Such means may well be efficacious even though they are intolerant and oppressive; and Locke, who is concerned only with the rationality of persecution, provides no argument against them.' (Waldron, 1988, p.81)

Waldron's argument draws attention to the fact that although coercion cannot work directly on the will, it can nevertheless be employed so as to support and foster certain sorts of beliefs rather than others. Persecutors need not be as direct and unsubtle as Locke imagines them to be. They may compel belief, not by threatening torture or imprisonment for unbelievers, but by restricting the availability of literature likely to shake belief. This would, in some circumstances, constitute coercing belief, albeit indirectly. So Locke is wrong, and belief can in fact be coerced, as every persecutor worth his salt has known all along. The charge here is not (as earlier) the simple charge of historical specificity, but of straightforward error.

Putting these thoughts together generates a two pronged attack on Locke's defence of religious toleration: some claim that it is so specific as to have outlived its usefulness. Others, like Waldron, claim that it was always flawed and therefore not very useful even in its own day. I shall concentrate on the latter point first, and suggest that Locke's claim that religious belief cannot be coerced incorporates an important truth which is ignored by Waldron and neglected in modern political philosophy generally. If I am right, modern accounts of toleration will be seen to be impoverished by their failure to do justice to Locke's argument.

Waldron's charge against Locke is that he ignores an important sense in which belief can be coerced – not directly, for sure, but indirectly. Such is the case when magistrates, politicians, people in authority generally, engage in censorship of a sort which will serve to suppress heterodox opinion. Thus, for example, governments anxious to suppress the belief that the earth is round might ban all books in which round-earth theories were promulgated. In consequence of this policy, it might be true both that people believe that the earth is flat and that that belief has been (indirectly) coerced. Plausible though it may appear, Waldron's account overlooks two important features of Locke's argument and of our own intuitions about the nature of commitment, particularly moral and religious commitment. The first is that coerced religious belief may be sincere but not authentic, even if the coercion is of the indirect and subtle kind mentioned above. This may be because the manner in which a belief is held, or the causal story which explains how it came to be held, are crucial to determining whether it counts as authentic. In other words, there may be an important distinction (in religious and moral cases) between the sincere utterance of a belief and the authenticity of that belief. Locke's argument, moreover, is not simply an argument about sincere belief but (crucially) an argument about authenticity. In what follows I shall try to explain this distinction between sincerity and authenticity, with particular reference to moral and religious cases.

In his article 'Deciding to Believe' Bernard Williams isolates four conditions which are necessary for authentic belief. Amongst these is what he calls the 'acceptance' condition. This condition dictates that for full blown belief we need both the possibility of deliberate reticence (not saying what I believe) and the possibility of insincerity (saying something other than what I believe). The point of the acceptance condition is to indicate that sincere utterance is neither a necessary nor a sufficient condition of belief: not necessary because we may choose to be reticent about our beliefs; not sufficient because the possibility of insincere utterance must be available to the speaker if it is to be appropriate to call him or her a believer (Williams, 1973, pp.136–51). Now depending on how certain beliefs are induced, it may be that this acceptance condition goes unsatisfied. Cases of hypnotism, for example, might be of this sort, as might cases of brain washing. When people have been hypnotised or subjected to brain-washing they are (characteristically) unable to say anything other than what they have been induced to say. Of course, the cases which Waldron envisages in which belief is indirectly coerced will not be of this dramatic sort, but they might nevertheless be cases where the acceptance condition is not met. Crucially, examples of this sort serve at least to cast doubt on the assumption that all that is required for authentic belief is sincere utterance plus a reputable causal story about how the belief was acquired. And it is this latter which Waldron assumes.

The notion of sincerity is also problematic in another way: people who have not been hypnotised or brain-washed, and who are not insincere in their utterances, may nevertheless be held not to believe that p despite the fact that they claim to believe that p. This is very often evident in professions of religious or moral belief, where people's deeds betray their genuine (authentic) beliefs more reliably than any statement of belief. People who sincerely and honestly claim not to be racially prejudiced may nevertheless act out their true beliefs in such a way as to undermine the professed beliefs.

The point of these considerations is not, I repeat, to deny Waldron's claim that coercion may work on the epistemic apparatus that surrounds belief, even if it cannot work on the state of belief itself. It is simply to resist the move from that claim to the claim that authentic belief is constituted only by sincere utterance plus a causal story. In claiming that 'only light can change Men's opinions', Locke is pointing to an important difficulty in the philosophy of mind, and one which has consequences for moral and political philosophy. This is, quite simply, that sincere utterance is not enough, whether in the expression of moral beliefs, or religious beliefs, or empirical propositions. There may, in all these cases, be a gap between the sincerity of the utterance and the genuineness or authenticity of the belief.

A further point arises here concerning the relationship between moral or religious beliefs and factual beliefs. The foregoing remarks have suggested that there is an important distinction between a belief's being sincerely uttered and its being authentic or genuine, and that this distinction applies equally to the case of religious belief and to the case of factual belief. Modern moral and political philosophy has tended to exaggerate the distinction between these two kinds of belief, and relatedly it has exaggerated the sense in which it is possible to choose or decide upon one's moral beliefs, often construing these choices as a matter of rationality. One important feature of Locke's claim that belief is not subject to the will is, I think, its implication that moral and religious belief are not, properly speaking, objects of choice at all. Again, Williams says:

> 'There are points of resemblance between moral and factual convictions; and I suspect it to be true of moral, as it certainly is of factual convictions that we cannot take very seriously a profession of them if we are given to understand that the speaker has just decided to adopt them . . . We see a man's genuine convictions as coming from somewhere deeper in him than that.' (p.227)

One point to be made here is that this way of talking about moral or religious beliefs assimilates them to factual beliefs (at least in part) and distances them from mere preferences or fancies. Even if we believe that God is dead, we still construe the religious believer as acknowledging something rather than opting for something in the expression of religious faith. (This interpretation of Locke is discussed in Passmore, 1986, pp.23–46).

Moreover, this way of looking at the problem is not wholly unfamiliar to us now, as can be seen by considering a recent justification of the English law of blasphemy. There it is held that the reason religious beliefs deserve special protection, over and above the protection afforded to other kinds of beliefs, is that religious belief is 'ultimate and compelling'. Ultimate in the sense that in a profession of religious faith a person states the most powerful conviction that it is possible to make. Compelling in the sense that sincere religious believers have no choice in the matter: they simply acknowledge what is for them an undeniable reality (Edwards, 1985, pp.75–98). Given this view of the matter, which is prevalent now as well as being encapsulated in Locke's account, the irrationality of coercing belief, even indirectly, is akin to the irrationality of brain washing: it can certainly be done, but it does not generate the right kind of belief or, more precisely, it does not generate a belief which is held in the right kind of way.

Obviously, there are great difficulties here which I have not even touched upon. It may be said, for instance, that in a sense we are all brainwashed, since we all are subject to selective sensory or other input which is causally related to the beliefs we sincerely hold. But it is one thing to say that all belief must be causally explicable, quite another to say that any causal explanation is as good as any other, and that all sincerely expressed beliefs are equally authentic. It is this latter point which Locke's argument reminds us of. However, even if it is admitted that the brainwashing argument will not do, there is another consideration which may serve to cast doubt on the criticism advanced against Locke. Earlier I summed up Jeremy Waldron's argument as issuing in the conclusion that belief can be indirectly coerced and that therefore Locke was wrong: persecutors have long known that whilst they cannot literally beat believers into submission, they can nevertheless use subtler means to induce the right beliefs. However, whilst this can be done, it is a strategy which looks more plausible when dealing with children, or with those who have no fully developed convictions. But Locke's argument precisely concerns the irrationality of such a strategy in a case where belief is strong. Here we should not underestimate the difficulty which will be involved in coercing belief, however subtly and indirectly.

One of the points made earlier about religious belief is that it is not only compelling, but also ultimate. It is the most powerful conviction that it is possible to make. Implicit in this is the recognition that it is a conviction which affects very many (if not all) aspects of life for the believer and that altering such beliefs will not simply be a matter of making the Bible inaccessible, for instance, or of implementing state subsidy of copies of Nietzsche. Religious belief will, and has, survived all that. That it has survived is in part because of the ultimate and all-pervasive nature of religious belief. Once you start, there is no end to the amount you have to pull down in order to coerce belief (or disbelief) and, to quote Williams again, though in a slightly different context 'it is like a revolutionary movement trying to extirpate the last remains of the ancien regime'. It is a huge task and one which cannot lightly be embarked upon. Since religious belief and profoundly held moral belief will inform and guide virtually everything a believer does, virtually everything will have to be dismantled if religious belief is to be stamped out or radically transformed.

This argument also indicates the differences between indirect coercion in the case of religious belief and indirect coercion in the case of preferences. It is, at least arguably, a rational strategy for governments to coerce better eating habits by, for example, subsidising wholemeal bread, or placing prohibitive taxes on refined sugar. But that is because eating habits do not, generally speaking, impinge upon and inform one's whole life. The task of coercing believers into a state of unbelief, however indirect and subtle, would be an altogether different enterprise. It would be not merely a more complex version of the dietary case, but a qualitatively different case altogether.

The upshot of the foregoing arguments is to suggest that there is something important and relevant in Locke's argument against religious intolerance: crudely put, Locke serves to remind us of the all-pervasive character of religious and moral belief in the life of the believer. In urging the irrationality of coercion he is certainly making a point about religious belief which has limited application in a secular society. But its limitations are not as great as they may sometimes seem to be. In multi-cultural and multi-racial societies such as twentieth-century Britain and America, many religious beliefs are profoundly held. If we are to refuse to extend toleration to the holders of such beliefs, then we must be clear about the enormity of what we are doing. Locke's point, even when stripped of its assumptions about the nature and importance of salvation, is that the task of obtaining genuine conformity in the areas of moral and religious belief is likely to be extremely difficult and to have far-reaching ramifications.

Reasons and consequences

The argument of the previous section suggests several senses in which Locke's insistence that belief is not subject to the will, and not something which can be coercively induced, is important for and acknowledged by modern attitudes to religious toleration. Firstly, it emphasises the distinction between sincere utterance and genuine or authentic belief. Secondly, it emphasises the all-pervasive nature of religious belief and the concomitant difficulties inherent in attempting to dismantle such belief. Finally, it emphasises how misleading it may be to speak of moral and religious beliefs as the objects of deliberate and rational choice. The appropriate terms here are sight-analogous terms – 'recognising', 'seeing', 'acknowledging', etc., not 'choosing', 'opting' or 'deciding'. In brief, Locke's account of the nature and status of religious belief fits ill with the 'smorgasbord' view of the diversity of life, which is so popular amongst many modern liberals.

This brings us to the second feature of Locke's account which is criticised by modern philosophers: his emphasis on the specific reasons which motivate intolerance, rather than on its practical consequences. Of course, Locke is not indifferent about *all* consequences of intolerance. In particular, and as we have already seen, he is concerned that toleration not be extended in cases where it will have dangerous or unsettling political consequences. Hence, for example, his insistence that toleration not be extended to Catholics or atheists. In Locke's view, Catholics are not to be trusted because they owe allegiance to a foreign power (the Pope), and atheists are not to be trusted because they owe allegiance to no one at all. Both groups are, therefore, equally untrustworthy from the magistrate's point of view, and equally likely to disrupt civil peace and harmony. In consequence, they are not proper recipients of religious toleration. Nevertheless, Locke adopts a reason-based account of toleration in just this sense – that this attack on intolerance and persecution is framed in terms of the reasons which persecutors may have for suppressing religious practices. Throughout the *Letter* he argues against irrationality in *motivation* and is indifferent as to whether members of religious sects are treated even-handedly or given equal opportunities within society. His exclusive concern is that (with the exception of Catholics and atheists) they not be discriminated against *for reasons of religion*, but he is silent about the many other reasons which there might be for intolerance. Thus, for example, he has nothing to say against political or economic reasons for suppressing certain sects, even though these may serve just as effectively as religious reasons to restrict the power and effectiveness of those sects. An example of this might be the repression or repatriation of immigrant Jews, not on grounds of their religion, but on the economic ground that the country cannot afford to offer them hospitality. Similarly, Locke will have no argument based on toleration against the suppression of certain religious practices just as long as those practices are restricted on grounds which are not religious.

At this point, it is worth recalling, and discussing in greater detail, the argument which he presents against banning the sacrifice, but not the slaughter of cattle;

'But if peradventure such were the state of things, that the Interest of the Commonwealth required all slaughter of Beasts should be forborn for some while, in order to the increasing of the stock of Cattel, that had been destroyed by some extraordinary Murrain; Who sees not that the Magistrate, in such a case, may forbid all his Subjects to kill any Calves for any use whatsoever? Only 'tis to be observed, that in this case the Law is not made about a Religious, but a Political matter: nor is the Sacrifice, but the Slaughter of Calves thereby prohibited.'

Locke's argument here is frequently thought to be an invitation to sophistry, for the effect of an economic ban on animal slaughter may be exactly the same as a ban that is religiously inspired. As Waldron remarks, 'Perhaps in both cases the religious sect will wither and die out as its congregation, deprived of their favourite ceremony, drift off to other faiths' (p.77). For reasons which I have already given, I doubt whether the decline of the sect would be quite as easily obtained as that, nor do I think it appropriate to describe the members of the religious sect as deprived of their favourite ceremony in much the same way as I might be deprived of my favourite television programme should the government think it necessary, for economic reasons, to impose power cuts. (Drifting to another faith is not, I think, like transferring allegiance from one soap opera to another.)

Nevertheless, the point remains that Locke is here advocating what has been called a 'principle of restraint' – that is, a principle which (in this case) defines religious liberty not by the actions permitted on the part of the person whose liberty is in question, but by the motivations it prohibits on the part of the person who is in a position to threaten liberty. Locke does not think that there is a right to freedom of worship as such, but only a right not to have one's worship interfered with for religious ends. He is, therefore, officially indifferent as to whether religious sects flourish or wither. This aspect of his account may be sharply distinguished from most modern liberalism and from Mill's views in *On Liberty*. These accounts characteristically construe diversity as a good in itself and urge a much more strenuous principle of restraint than does Locke.

There is, therefore, a significant gulf which separates the aim of much modern liberalism from the political theory of Locke's *Letter*. Locke has no commitment to diversity, no belief in the inherent goodness of varieties of ways of life, and no argument for the preservation of religious sub groups within the dominant culture of a society. Again, his point is simply that it would be irrational to suppress them, not that it would be morally wrong. In considering this point, I shall not attempt to deny the sophistry which it potentially invites. Rather, I shall draw attention to some significant ways in which Locke's account is superior to Mill's (and is so despite its tendency to invite sophistry). This, I hope, will pave the way to the discussion of Mill's arguments which will form the basis of the next chapter.

The first point to make is that Locke's argument is a quite specific argument for toleration, or against persecution (he standardly takes the two as identical). Unlike Mill, and many modern liberals, Locke is not providing an argument for liberty generally. This is not an unimportant point, for there are two distinct and separable questions here: the first is 'What rights do I have to pursue my own way of life and ideals?' The second question is 'What obligations do others have to desist from preventing me from pursuing my own way of life and ideals?' That these two are separable will be argued for in the next section. All I wish to do here is to draw attention to the fact that where Mill is arguing for liberty, Locke is arguing against intolerance, and to suggest that that fact alone may make an important difference to our assessment of their respective theories.

The second point to be made is that Locke's insistence on neutrality about reasons is something which meshes in with our own practice in modern society in at least one area. This is the area of race relations. The race relations acts in Britain hold precisely that people must be neutral as regards the reasons they have for preventing people of other races from doing certain kinds of things – namely that those reasons must not include the reason that they belong to that particular race. Thus, the law does not require total even-handedness; it requires only neutrality with respect to reasons, and it does this by reference to what racial discrimination definitionally is, i.e. treating one person less favourably than another on grounds of race.

Similarly with religious intolerance or persecution. This is, by definition, treating one person less favourably than another on grounds of religion. Further laws, for example laws requiring equal opportunities or reverse discrimination, or affirmative action, may well be (and in my view are) highly desirable, but they may not be laws whose rationale is primarily a concern for toleration. It follows from this that the argument for specifically religious toleration presented in the *Letter* need not require in Locke an indifference as to whether religious groups flourish or wither. It requires only that the demands of toleration lead so far and no further.

This point will be of increasing importance in later chapters of this book where modern defences of toleration are discussed, for part of my argument there will be that the more modest aims adopted by Locke may be all that we can reasonably expect of a theory of toleration. In so far as modern liberals expect more, they have, I shall suggest, unreasonable expectations. In particular, modern liberalism has often manifested its own inconsistency, or even duplicity, in urging more extensive neutrality or even-handedness. Unlike Locke, modern liberals frequently urge neutrality with respect to the outcome of actions and, like Lord Scarman, often imply that in the twentieth century toleration requires more than merely 'letting alone'. It requires aiding, assisting and fostering. It seems to me doubtful whether such complete even-handedness is a possible aim, and even more doubtful whether it is justifiable in the name of toleration. I shall say no more about this here except to recall a remark by Professor Cranston to the effect that Locke, in the *Letter on Toleration*, is advocating reasonableness in the ordering of society (Cranston, 1987, p.121). This is not, as Cranston points out, an ideal which we attain today in what we tolerate and what we don't. Perhaps part of the reason for this is an excessive commitment to the unattainable ideal of neutrality. That possibility will be explored in the chapters which follow. Another possibility will be explored in the final section of this chapter.

Tolerated and tolerators

The final feature of Locke's account to which I shall draw attention is its bias towards considering not the rights of the tolerated (the rights of the victims of persecution), but the rationality of the would-be perpetrators of intolerance. The criticism made of this way of proceeding is that it fails properly to acknowledge what is most objectionable about instances of intolerance, namely that intolerance frequently constitutes a violation of individual rights. Much modern political theory proceeds by outlining the rights which people may properly be said to have and then urging that these rights not be violated. Locke, of course, is no stranger to the notion of individual rights, but in the *Letter on Toleration* he concentrates exclusively on the obligations of the magistrates and says little about the rights of the tolerated. Indeed, and as has been mentioned already, the *Letter* contains no general argument for a right to freedom of worship at all.

In the previous section I referred to two distinct but related questions which we may ask in this area: the question 'What rights do I have to pursue my own way of life and ideals?' and the question 'What obligations do others have to desist from preventing me pursuing my own way of life and ideals?' Much the greater part of modern philosophy has concentrated on the former of the two questions, and it is Locke's failure to do so which makes him the target of criticism here. Recently, however, Onora O'Neill has suggested that there is much to be said for reminding ourselves of the latter question (O'Neill, 'Practices of Toleration' unpublished paper). The reasons for this are not wholly sympathetic to Locke's own case, but they do provide a warning of the dangers of pursuing rights theories too vigorously. Again, all I wish to do is to suggest that the assumption that everything can be explained if we concentrate on victims' rights is far too simplistic, and that in so far as this is the charge against Locke, it is ill-founded. It may be better to adopt Locke's general strategy and concentrate on the obligations we have, rather than on the rights others have.

The burden of O'Neill's argument is that when considering questions of toleration a difficulty arises if we concern ourselves only with rights. This difficulty is that if we allow only negative rights (rights not to be killed, not to be interfered with against our will), then we are forced to the conclusion that as long as no right is violated, there is nothing wrong with the policy we are pursuing. Conversely, if we allow more extensive, welfare rights (rights to be given aid and assistance in various forms), then we encounter the difficulty that there is no way of identifying a unique, maximal set of mutually consistent rights. Since rights can be cashed out in terms of obligations, it follows that welfare rights theorists will risk imposing inconsistent obligations on people. By contrast, proponents of negative rights retain consistency but the price is that they fail to say what is wrong with a whole range of actions which appear to be very wrong indeed.

The remedy for this, O'Neill suggests, is to remind ourselves that the perspective of rights is only one perspective in liberal political theory and that the alternative perspective, that of obligation, may serve us better in discussions of toleration. What lies behind this thought is the belief that, whilst rights can be exhaustively analysed in terms of obligations, the converse is not the case and therefore the perspective of obligation may enable us to explain why certain actions are wrong even though they do not constitute a violation of rights. The specific question of toleration, which actions are to be permitted even though they are wrong, and which actions are both wrong and impermissible is, of course, a separate and further one. All that is being suggested here is that a motivation exists for us, and for Locke, to turn to the perspective of obligation when once we realise that neither libertarian rights nor welfare rights can serve adequately to explain our attitude to various forms of disagreeable behaviour.

This, I believe, is an insight which lies at the heart of Locke's discussion of toleration: there may be no general right to freedom of worship, but still there is something very wrong with religious persecution. For reasons which have already been discussed, Locke pinpoints the wrongness as lying in the irrationality of attempting to coerce religious belief, but it would be a mistake to conclude (as Waldron does) that 'having shown why intolerance is irrational, Locke thinks himself excused from the messy business of explaining the reasons why it is wrong'. Quite the reverse, for the moral wrongess of intolerance consists precisely in its irrationality.

This moral wrongness may be explained in two ways: firstly, and as already indicated, Locke's Puritanism dictates the moral necessity of behaving rationally. Secondly, and crucially, however, the magistrate who attempts to coerce religious belief acts morally wrongly in that he exceeds his brief. To recall, the role of the magistrate is to preserve civil peace, not to save souls. 'These considerations, to omit many others that might have been urged to the same purpose, seem unto me sufficient to conclude that all the Power of Civil Government relates only to Men's Civil Interests, is confined to the care of the things of this World, and hath nothing to do with the World to come' (p.28). The magistrate thus has a moral obligation to desist from interfering in matters religious, even though the individual has no right to freedom of worship as such. By throwing emphasis onto rationality, Locke is not denying or ignoring the moral wrongness of intolerance. Rather, he is gesturing towards the fact that an action may be wrong even though it violates no right. In particular, it may be wrong when it constitutes evidence of the agent's neglect of his own duties and failure to recognise the boundaries of his jurisdiction. Modern philosophy does indeed concentrate on the rights of the persecuted rather than the duties of the would-be persecutors. In this sense, Locke's analysis may appear somewhat strange to our eyes. But unless and until we have a more coherent account of rights, we should be wary of dismissing out of hand alternative explanations such as this.

Concluding remarks

It has been the aim of this chapter to suggest that there is
something worthwhile in Locke's treatment of religious toleration.
Specifically, Locke's insistence that religious belief cannot be
coerced points to a distinction between sincere and authentic belief
which is of particular relevance in the religious case, but which
also has application to profoundly held moral belief. It reminds
us that for the religious believer, the assertion of faith is more
akin to an assertion of factual belief, an acknowledgement of an
inescapable truth, than to a rational choice or preference.
Moreover, it points to the all-pervasive nature of moral and
religious belief: to the ultimate and compelling nature of those
beliefs which may be such as to infuse a person's entire life.
Crucially, it reminds us that there is an important sense in which
moral and religious beliefs are not themselves choices, they are
the things which inform and dictate choices.

Secondly, Locke's emphasis on reasons draws attention to the
distinction between the concept of toleration and the concepts of
liberty or equality. It likewise warns us against exaggerated
optimism in our attempts to attain official neutrality, and points
the way to a defence of toleration which, unlike Mill's defence,
and unlike many modern liberal defences, is not simply part of a
more general argument for liberty. In brief, Locke makes clear
the distinction between the concept of toleration (which involves
necessary reference to that which is undesirable or unwanted),
and associated concepts, such as liberty. His argument attempts
to explain exactly how much we may require in the name of
toleration, and how much must be the province of different
arguments.

Finally, Locke's move from the perspective of rights to the
perspective of obligations is not thereby a denial of the wrongs
done to the victims of intolerance, but a reminder of the difficulties
attendant upon supposing both that we must aim for internal
consistency in our moral theories, and that there are some wrongs
which are not violations of rights. Locke's emphasis on rationality
is greater than and different from that which is favoured in modern
moral philosophy, for it incorporates necessary reference to moral
obligation. Moreover, in assessing Locke's theory we should not
assume that consistency, rationality and reasonableness have no

force, simply because we believe that they do not have quite the force Locke believed them to have. Most importantly, we should not reject his theory as too minimalist or too pragmatic until we have examined more extensive theories and established whether they can provide better arguments than those incorporated in the *Letter*.

In the next chapter I shall discuss one such theory – the theory advanced by John Stuart Mill in his essay *On Liberty*. My claim will be that, in the final analysis, Mill's account is less coherent and plausible than Locke's, even though it may appear superior at first glance.

3 Mill and the Case for Diversity

The Beehive State and The Chinese Lady's Foot

John Stuart Mill's essay *On Liberty* is one of the most important, yet puzzling and controversial works in the whole corpus of political philosophy. Published in February of 1859, it purports to present and defend 'one very simple principle' and to serve one single purpose. It is, in Mill's own words, 'a philosophic text book of a single truth . . . the importance, to man and society, of a large variety in types of character, and of giving full freedom to human nature to expand itself in innumerable and conflicting directions'. It urges the importance of individual freedom in face of 'the despotism of custom' and 'the demand that all other people should resemble ourselves'. It warns against 'dulling conformity' and 'the Chinese ideal of making all people alike'. It inveighs against 'the tyranny of public opinion' and advocates eccentricity as the only means of breaking that tyranny. It is, in brief, a paean of praise to unbridled individuality and human diversity (Mill, 1978).

This brief outline already indicates some of the great differences which divide Mill's theory from Locke's. Firstly, Mill's argument is much wider in scope than is Locke's: where Locke is concerned with the specific problem of religious toleration, Mill is presenting a quite general case for liberty. As we have already seen, Locke's thesis contains no commitment to the value of diversity as such (whether in religious or other spheres), whereas Mill's argument is crucially an argument about the importance of allowing, and even encouraging, extensive diversity. Locke's argument concentrates on specifically legal restrictions on religious belief and practice, whereas Mill's account also considers the problem of social intolerance – intolerance in the form of the despotism of custom or the tyranny of the majority. In short, Mill is putting forward a general and positive case for liberty and the importance of diversity, whereas Locke is advancing a specific and negative case against religious persecution.

From the beginning, the book generated controversy: James Fitzjames Stephen briskly rejected it with the statement; 'There is hardly anything in the whole essay which can properly be called proof as distinguished from enunciation or assertion . . . I think, however, that it will not be difficult to show that the principle stands in much need of proof' (Fitzjames Stephen, 1967, p.56). Yet more damning was the *Dublin Review*, which robustly asserted 'had Mr. Mill's character depended on this essay alone he would never have acquired the reputation of "a logical, consistent intellect"', while Caroline Fox referred to it as 'that terrible book, so clear, and calm, and cold . . . Mill makes me shiver, his blade is so keen and unhesitating.'

The contemporary reception of *On Liberty* was not, however, entirely negative: Buckle declared it to be a 'noble treatise, so full of wisdom and of thought', and the *Saturday Review* stated 'we know of nothing in English literature since *Areopagitica* more stirring, more noble, better worthy of the most profound and earnest meditation' (as quoted in Rees, 1985, p.79). Whatever virtues it may have lacked, and whatever defects it may have displayed, *On Liberty* was nothing if not controversial.

In modern political theory, controversy about the intellectual calibre of *On Liberty* takes the form of disputes about its consistency rather than about its truth. In particular, it is often doubted whether the text is internally consistent: Mill may present a simple principle but, it is claimed, the arguments which he adduces in support of that principle are confused and conflicting. Moreover, it is unclear what place is occupied by *On Liberty* in the corpus of Mill's writings. Does it cohere with his earlier utilitarianism, or does it signal a departure from the doctrine and from his early Benthamite beliefs? Are there really two Mills – the Mill of *Utilitarianism* and the Mill of *On Liberty*? (Rees, 1985, Himmelfarb, 1974, Mazlish, 1975, Robson, 1968). What exactly is the simple principle of *On Liberty*? What are its philosophical underpinnings and how is it to be interpreted and applied? Is it really, as Mill says, an application of the principle of utility, or is it a separate and incompatible principle? I raise these questions in order to indicate the complexity of the text, and the difficulties inherent in any attempt to analyse it. The supposedly 'simple principle' is far from simple either in interpretation or application. Therefore, like all other analyses of it, what follows will be controversial and tentative.

My strategy in this chaper will be as follows: I shall (somewhat artificially) divide Mill's text into a positive and a negative component. The positive component is his argument in favour of liberty; the negative component, his justification of restrictions on liberty. I shall then compare the scope and structure of his argument for liberty with Locke's argument for toleration. This comparison will pave the way to a critique of Mill's liberalism and its philosophical foundations. My conclusion will be that Mill's argument is flawed in a way which has important consequences for liberalism generally and for modern liberalism in particular: the unspoken presuppositions of his theory should make us sceptical about the possibility of finding a genuinely liberal defence of toleration.

The simple principle: positive and negative

So far, I have spoken in very general terms of the principle of *On Liberty* as a principle of individuality, diversity and eccentricity. Mill takes as the motto for the book a passage from Von Humboldt's *Sphere and Duties of Government*;

> 'The grand, leading principle, towards which every argument unfolded in these pages directly converges, is the absolute and essential importance of human development in its richest diversity.'

This, however, is the general theme of the book. Its text, the statement of the principle itself, is more specific: it not only praises diversity, but also aspires to provide a practical criterion for deciding the scope and limits of societal interference in individual liberty. Mill says;

> 'The object of this essay is to assert one very simple principle,

as entitled to govern absolutely the dealings of society with the individual in the way of compulsion and control, whether the means used be physical force in the form of legal penalties or the moral coercion of public opinion. That principle is that the sole end for which mankind are warranted, individually or collectively, in interfering with the liberty of action of any of their number is self-protection. That the only purpose for which power can be rightfully exercised over any member of a civilised community, against his will, is to prevent harm to others. His own good, either physical or moral, is not a sufficient warrant. He cannot rightfully be compelled to do or forbear because it will be better for him to do so, because it will make him happier, because, in the opinions of others, to do so would be wise or even right. These are good reasons for remonstrating with him, or reasoning with him, or persuading him, or entreating him, but not for compelling him or visiting him with any evil in case he do otherwise. To justify that, the conduct from which it is desired to deter him must be calculated to produce evil to someone else. The only part of the conduct of anyone for which he is amenable to society is that which concerns others. In the part which merely concerns himself, his independence is, of right, absolute. Over himself, over his own mind and body, the individual is sovereign.' (pp.68–9).

This lengthy, but definitive statement of the 'simple principle' of *On Liberty* illustrates the positive and negative components of Mill's theory. On the positive side, he is presenting an argument for the freedom of the individual from coercion and constraint by society. On the negative side, he is citing the necessary (but not sufficient) conditions for restricting that freedom. Broadly, his claim is that individual freedom is supremely important and may be restricted only in order to prevent harm to others. (It is important to note here that Mill is not claiming that interference is justified in all cases where an action will result in harm to others. His point is simply that it is in such cases alone that the *question* of interference arises. Thus, even where an action will result in harm to others, it may still be that interference is not warranted.)

By separating these positive and negative components, we may divide discussion of Mill's account into two parts: firstly an investigation of his grounds for giving such prominence to liberty (that will be the aim of this chapter), and secondly an examination of the limits of liberty (that question will be discussed in more general terms in Chapter 5). John Rees explains the connection between the two as follows; 'The book deals with one of the recurring questions of politics, but was written in circumstances which gave that question new significance. For behind Mill's question – "What is the nature and extent of the power which society ought to exercise over the individual?" – was his anxiety lest the tendencies which he claimed to see at work in the civilised world would eventually extinguish spontaneity in all the important branches of human conduct' (p.137). Thus the negative component of Mill's work (his statement of restrictions on liberty) is an attempt to provide *practical* criteria for safeguarding individual diversity and sovereignty. But what is the argument which justifies its positive component – its insistence on the importance of individual sovereignty and spontaneity?

Like Locke, Mill was influenced in his philosophical writings by the circumstances prevailing in his own society. His conceptual claims about individuality and the importance of diversity are prompted by reflections on the customs and mores of European, and particularly British, society in the mid-nineteenth century. Additionally, de Tocqueville's *Democracy in America* exerted a powerful influence upon him and increased his conviction that tyranny could be exercised by the will of the people, and that individuality must therefore be safeguarded.

This theme, foreshadowed in several earlier essays, reached maturity in *On Liberty*. In the opening chapter of that essay he reflects upon the tendency of people to impose their own opinions and inclinations on others. This tendency, he says, is not declining but growing in nineteenth-century Britain and Europe, and 'unless a strong barrier of moral conviction can be raised against the mischief, we must expect, in the present circumstances of the world, to see it increase.' Mill's claim is not simply that the legal powers of the state are increasing and limiting individuals' capacity for spontaneous action. He emphasises even more the informal and social forces which he thinks are at work. In Chapter III, 'Of Individuality', he inveighs against 'the despotism of custom' which, he claims, 'proscribes singularity' and allows change only on condition that all change together: 'everyone must still dress like other people, but the fashion may change once or twice a year.'

'The depotism of custom is everywhere the standing hindrance to human advancement,' says Mill, and he concludes, 'the modern *regime* of public opinion is, in an unorganized form, what the Chinese educational and political systems are in an organized; and unless individuality shall be able successfully to assert itself against this yoke, Europe . . . will tend to become another China' (p.138).

The Chinese practice of foot binding symbolised for Mill all that was to be feared in the suppression of individuality by the despotism of custom. It implied the imposition of uniformity, the stunting of natural growth (both physical and moral), and the dreariness of a world which contained nothing new or different or exciting. 'Its ideal of character is to be without any marked character – to maim by compression, like a Chinese lady's foot, every part of human nature which stands out prominently and tends to make the person markedly dissimilar in outline to commonplace humanity' (p.135).

Many contemporary commentators took exception to Mill's claim that nineteenth-century Europe was poised at the top of a slippery slope which led inexorably to this 'Chinese ideal' of uniformity. Their observations led them to believe that diversity was increasing, not declining. They pointed to the increased freedom of women, to the growth of religious freedom, and to the freedom to choose the education of one's children as evidence of this. Some even cited Mill's own popularity as proof that individuality was not scorned. Mill was wrong about the facts. He was, in Macaulay's words, 'crying "Fire!" in Noah's flood' (as quoted in Thomas, 1985, p.104).

But whatever the facts of the matter, Mill's commitment to diversity, and his enthusiasm for eccentricity were also conceptually puzzling. Why should diversity be thought good in itself? What was the value of mere eccentricity for its own sake? Fitzjames Stephen was forthright on the subject. Commenting on 'the odd manner in which Mr. Mill worships mere variety' he remarked, 'A nation in which everyone was sober would be a happier, better, and more progressive, though a less diversified nation than one of which half the members were sober and the other half habitual drunkards' (Stephen, p.83). The point retains its force: enthusiasm for diversity, individuality and eccentricity stand in need of justification, and whatever Mill's fears about the tyranny of public opinion and the despotism of custom, it is a large step from that to unqualified enthusiasm for diversity of all and any sort. But is it true, as Fitzjames Stephen claims, that Mill worships 'mere variety'? There are a number of reasons for thinking that he does not, and that his argument for liberty and diversity is explicable by reference to other values.

The value of diversity

As we have seen, Mill makes frequent and disparaging references to the 'Chinese ideal of making all people alike', and to the tendency (as he saw it) in nineteenth-century Europe to impose uniformity either by legal restrictions or by social pressures. This growth of state and societal interference was anathema to him, and it was so for one very important reason: it implied a theory of human nature which Mill believed to be both false and pernicious. 'There is no reason at all' he says 'that human existence should be constructed on some one or some small number of patterns. If a person possesses any tolerable amount of common sense and experience, his own mode of laying out his existence is best, not because it is the best in itself, but because it is his own mode. Human beings are not like sheep, and even sheep are not undistinguishably alike' (pp.132–3). And again, 'Human nature is not a machine to be built after a model, and set to do exactly the work prescribed for it, but a tree, which requires to grow and develop itself on all sides, according to the tendency of the inward forces which make it a living thing' (p.123).

Mill's rejection of the 'Chinese ideal' is premised on a belief in individual diversity, coupled with an organic view of human nature, according to which different sorts of people will find their natural growth and fulfilment in different ways. There may be no more reason why two different people should flourish in the same moral climate than why the daffodil and the orchid should flourish in the same physical climate. To impose a single manner of living on people of different constitutions would be just as stunting as to impose (by binding) a single size on Chinese ladies' feet. Moreover, it does not matter whether the imposition is the result of legal intervention or of social pressure. The result in either case is the same – an unnatural stunting of individuality. Thus, in addition to fears about the dreariness of a world of uniformity, Mill also bases his case for diversity on the essentially diverse character of human nature. Diversity is not an unargued good in itself, nor is it merely an aesthetic preference on Mill's part, it is also an important fact about human beings and therefore a necessary precondition of human flourishing.

To take an example not unlike that used by Fitzjames Stephen: we may think (though we need not) that the world would be a better place if there were no homosexuals in it. However, to suppress (by legal or social disapproval) the practice of homosexuality would be to stunt the very nature of those individuals themselves. It would be the moral equivalent of foot binding. We should therefore be wary of rejecting those forms of diversity which we dislike, or of which we disapprove, not because diversity is an inexplicable 'good in itself', but because it is an inevitable concomitant of the diversity of human beings themselves.

Of course nothing follows from this about the propriety of allowing all and any sort of diversity, and Mill himself is clear that there are limits to diversity (nothing in *On Liberty* commits him to favouring liberty for pyromaniacs, or rapists). All that follows is that commitment to diversity is not an ungrounded and inexplicable preference on his part. It is an ineradicable feature of human nature, and for that reason alone we should be loath to stifle or restrict it. This brings us on to a second, and slightly different, reason for Mill's commitment to diversity. In a passage quoted earlier in this section he says that a person's own mode of laying out his existence is best 'not because it is best in itself, but because it is his own mode'. This passage introduces a concept central to Mill's positive thesis in *On Liberty*, the concept of autonomy or self-determination. Although Mill does not himself use the term 'autonomy' it is this concept to which he is appealing in the positive argument of his text. The defence of diversity and the concomitant justifications of liberty and toleration are dependent upon the value which Mill places on individual autonomy.

The argument from autonomy states that it matters more that people should find their own route to the best way of life than that they should lead the best way of life. Immediately after his statement of the principle of liberty Mill says;

'It is, perhaps, hardly necessary to say that this doctrine is meant to apply only to human beings in the maturity of their faculties

. . . as soon as mankind have attained the capacity of being
guided to their own improvement by conviction or persuasion,
. . . compulsion, either in the direct form or in that of pains and
penalties for noncompliance, is no longer admissible as a means
to their own good, and justifiable only for the security of others.'
(p.69)

Implicit in this distinction between those to whom the principle of
liberty applies, and those who are outside its jurisdiction, is Mill's
commitment to the importance of autonomous choice: to force or
compel people to lead a particular way of life is not only to deform
their natural character, it is also, implicitly, to deny their status as
adult human beings.

The ideal of life for adults is self-government and self-direction –
to be an adult consists in making one's own decisions, choosing
one's own projects and determining one's own future. It consists
in making autonomous choices. Force and compulsion serve not
simply to deform the natural character of the agent, but also to
deny that he or she is an agent at all. They reduce the adult to a
child. In *The Subjection of Women* Mill refers to just this fact to
explain what is wrong with the position of women in Victorian
Britain. He says, 'All women are brought up from the very earliest
years in the belief that their ideal of character is the very opposite
to that of men; not self-will and government by self-control, but
submission and yielding to the control of others' (Mill, 1983, p.27).
In order that women be released from this subjection it is
imperative that they too be treated as autonomous, self-directing
beings. Thus, one reason for advocating the widest possible
liberty and for encouraging diversity, is that these are necessary
conditions for the development of that autonomy which is the
characteristic feature of the adult and which alone makes life
valuable for those who have arrived at the maturity of their
faculties.

But given that autonomy is so important a feature of adult life,
what exactly does it consist in, and how is it to be fostered and
developed? To answer this question, we shall need to examine
modern accounts of the concept and compare them with the
doctrine advanced by Mill.

The importance of autonomy

The concept of autonomy is most commonly associated with the eighteenth-century German philosopher, Immanuel Kant. In Kant's philosophy it is connected with a whole range of metaphysical and epistemological doctrines which Mill certainly did not share. Nevertheless, if we abstract from these doctrines, we find that, in modern philosophy, the guiding idea of an autonomous agent is of one who acts in obedience to a law which he has prescribed for himself. In modern language, the autonomous agent is self-governing and self-directed, in control of his (or her) own will and not subject to irresistible phobias, addictions, or passions.

This characterisation captures three crucial features of the concept of autonomy: firstly, the autonomous agent must be in a position to act. He must not be compelled by external forces such as torture or the threat of legal punishment. Secondly, the autonomous agent must not be pathologically driven by desires or compelled by irresistible urges which are such as to undermine his rationality. He must, in short, be a rational free chooser, not a psychopath or a drug addict whose addiction renders him incapable of free choice. Thirdly, and most importantly, the autonomous agent must *himself* prescribe the law to which he is obedient: in addition to being independent of others' coercive actions, he must also be independent of their will. Thus, the agent who conforms, more or less unthinkingly, to the custom and practice of his day, may be said not to be properly autonomous, since his will is determined by the will of those around him.

These three defining features of autonomy indicate why it is incompatible both with legal restrictions on action and with 'the despotism of custom' and the tyranny of the majority. Autonomy requires not only that the agent shall possess the standard negative liberties – freedom from constraint, coercion and the threat of punishment – but also freedom from the suffocating oppression of social mores and customs. These latter are a threat to and an infringement of individual autonomy in just the same way as legal restrictions. Arguably, they are an even greater infringement, for they serve to alter not only the agent's external behaviour, but also his opinion of himself and his own actions. They force the grown adult into the position of a child. They brow-beat him into conformity and submission, until eventually, like the child, he has no will of his own, but is moulded and fashioned by the will of others. To coerce people in this way is, implictly, to deny their status as autonomous agents, or rational free choosers. Mill's attack on the tyranny of opinion is therefore one indication that his primary concern, in advocating diversity, is the protection of autonomy, which may be threatened by social constraint just as much as (if not more than) it is threatened by legal restriction.

An important consequence of the autonomy argument is that it implies the need for a society which is plural and diverse. Mill believes that fully autonomous agents will display a high degree of diversity (since human nature is diverse), but it is also true that the development of autonomy requires diversity, for if being autonomous is being author of one's own life, then we can become authors of our own lives only on the assumption that we have an adequate range of acceptable alternatives from which to choose. Without this, human nature withers and autonomy becomes impossible. Mill describes the situation thus;

> 'The mind itself is bowed to the yoke: even in what people do for pleasure, conformity is the first thing thought of; they live in crowds, they exercise choice only amongst things commonly done; peculiarity of taste, eccentricity of conduct are shunned equally with crimes, until by dint of not following their own nature, they have no nature to follow; their human capacities are withered and starved; they become incapable of any strong wishes or native pleasures and are generally without either opinions or feelings of home growth or properly their own.' (Mill, 1978, pp.125–6)

They are, in brief, non-autonomous, and their autonomy is denied not by legal constraint, but by social pressures to conform – in other words, by the despotism of custom. Again, social pressure would deny them the opportunity to 'be who they are'.

This brief defence of Mill has so far taken the form of an explanation of his commitment to liberty and diversity. It has been suggested that, far from being merely an oddity, this commitment is firmly grounded in two more fundamental beliefs: the belief that human nature is diverse and can only flourish if allowed to express itself in all its diversity, and the belief in individual autonomy, which dictates that the life worth living is, supremely, the life which is self-chosen and self-determined. Such a life cannot be obtained or sustained in the absence of an adequate range of options, and thus diversity is a precondition of autonomy. In the language of modern political theory, Mill is justifying liberty and toleration by reference to autonomy, and he is insisting that the attainment of autonomy requires pluralism.

Locke, Mill and the tolerant society

We are now in a position to see more clearly the differences which divide Locke's defence of toleration from Mill's defence of liberty. In discussing Locke's account, I noted three areas in which his argument is held to be defective: it concentrates on the irrationality of intolerance, not on its immorality. It addresses itself to the perpetrators of intolerance, but says nothing about the wrong done to its victims. Finally, it emphasises the illegitimacy of appealing to religious reasons to justify intolerance, but has no argument against intolerance engaged in for other reasons. In each of these respects, Mill's account is thought to be superior to Locke's. It explains the immorality of intolerance as well as its irrationality. It accounts for the moral wrong done to the victims of intolerance, and it provides a quite general argument for extensive toleration, not an argument which depends upon the illegitimacy of specific reasons in the religious case only. These differences between Locke and Mill are significant in two respects: firstly, they remind us of the fact that the two writers are addressing slightly different questions. Secondly, they draw attention to Mill's uniquely important place as a defender of liberty within the liberal tradition.

In the chapter on Locke I noted that the alleged defects in his defence of toleration have prompted some commentators to deem it philosophically 'dead'. However, I also suggested that there are reasons for extending greater sympathy to his account than is normally offered. One reason is that Locke, unlike Mill, is dealing specifically with the problem of religious toleration, not with the larger question of liberty. Questions of toleration are, by definition, questions about how we should respond to things which we dislike, find distasteful, or morally wrong. By contrast, in discussions of liberty there need be no such implication.

This distinction between toleration and liberty will have consequences for the kinds of argument which can be expected in each case: considerations of liberty may be more far-reaching and may demand more of us than considerations of toleration. An argument for liberty, based upon belief in diversity and the value of autonomy, may require more than the simple neutrality with respect to reasons embodied in Locke's account: it may require fostering and encouraging diverse forms of life as a necessary precondition of the development and maintenance of autonomy. By contrast, toleration may simply involve accommodating those diverse forms of life which already exist.

The distinctions between Locke and Mill are thus, in part, a function of the fact that they are addressing different questions: Locke is asking the question 'What obligations do we have to desist from preventing people pursuing the way of life they deem best?' Whereas Mill is asking the question 'What rights do people have to pursue the way of life they think best?' Of course, the two questions are not unconnected. They are, nevertheless, distinct. If we are embarking on the Lockean project of dissuading people from acts of intolerance, then an argument designed to show their irrationality is powerful. If, on the other hand, we are engaged in the wider and more positive enterprise of showing that people are entitled to lead their own lives in their own way, then Mill's autonomy-based defence may be more appropriate. In this context, a defence of toleration will appear, not on its own, but as part of a wider defence of individual liberty.

The second point to be noted is that Mill's autonomy-based defence of liberty and toleration occupies an important place in the liberal tradition and provides crucial clues to the solution of the paradox of toleration. The precise connections between liberalism and the value of toleration will be discussed in the next chapter, but it is worth noting here that appeal to autonomy is not simply one argument amongst others for toleration. On the contrary, the autonomy argument is sometimes referred to as *the* characteristically liberal argument for toleration, the one argument not available to theorists from other traditions (Raz, 1986).

Liberalism, both historically and now, begins from a premise of individual diversity: each person has his unique conception of what makes life worth living and is entitled to pursue that conception to the best of his ability. Of course, and as we shall see, there are grave difficulties inherent in spelling out the precise implications of this premise, but in so far as that is the starting point of liberalism, the autonomy-based justification seems uniquely suited to it. By contrast, socialism and Marxism are characteristically presented as antipathetic to the concept of autonomy. What is important for them is not variety and self-determination, but moral consensus, and their view of human nature implies not diversity, but a very restricted and uniform notion of what can count as the rational ends of human beings.

Another way of expressing the point is by appeal to the paradox of toleration referred to in the first chapter. Toleration, in the strong sense, involves allowing things believed to be morally wrong. But if something is wrong, it is asked, how can it be right to allow it? The argument from autonomy provides at least the beginnings of an answer to this question: we should tolerate things believed to be wrong because we are interested not only in what people do, but also in the reasons they have for doing those things. Thus it is (in general) more important that people act autonomously than that they act correctly. Making choices for oneself (choosing autonomously) is more important than making right choices (choosing correctly). Autonomy provides a justification of toleration and also helps resolve the paradox of toleration. As Mill puts it, 'It really is of importance, not only what men do, but also what manner of men they are that do it' (Mill, 1978, p.123).

It follows from all this that, even if Locke's argument is not philosophically dead, it is nevertheless an argument which lacks the philosophical power and influence of Mill's. In particular, in so far as it concentrates on irrationality, and says little if anything about immorality, it fails to provide a justification of toleration springing from the inherent nature of persons themselves. By contrast, Mill's whole enterprise is designed to highlight the fact that intolerance constitutes a denial of the essential nature of human beings. This, of course, has a dark side: the success of Mill's enterprise depends crucially on his being right about human nature and the good for man. If he is wrong, then his account may prove to be far more illiberal than it first appears.

Autonomy and perfectibility: the case against Mill

The comparison between Mill's defence of liberty and Locke's

defence of religious toleration draws attention to the centrality of
the concept of autonomy (self-determination) in both historical
and modern liberalism. The autonomy-based argument which Mill
appeals to has been described as *the* specifically liberal argument
for toleration. If this is true, then (both for Mill and for us) much
hangs on the possibility of presenting a fully coherent analysis of
autonomy and of its role in justifying the liberal commitment to
toleration.

In this section I will look more closely at Mill's argument from
autonomy. My claim will be that it is, in many ways, Janus-faced
and that, when properly understood, it will be seen to have
implications quite at odds with its official liberal credentials: Mill
can be saved from the criticisms levelled by Fitzjames Stephen
and other contemporaries, but ironically he cannot be saved from
the illiberal implications of his own theory. Moreover, I shall
suggest in the next chapter that these faults are not easily rectified
by modern liberal theory. The flaws in Mill's doctrine spill over
into modern liberalism and render it incapable of delivering on its
promise of a truly diverse, open and tolerant society. Thus, a
critique of Mill's account is important both in itself and in its
consequences for us. It may prompt us to return to a more
minimalist, Lockian conception of toleration, or it may prompt us
to look for justifications of toleration outside the liberal tradition.

So far, two important features of Mill's defence of liberty have
been noted: his belief that diversity is morally required because
human nature is itself diverse ('human beings are not like sheep
and even sheep are not undistinguishably alike'); and his belief
that diversity is required as a necessary precondition of the
promotion and maintenance of autonomy ('It is the privilege and
proper condition of a human being arrived at the maturity of his
faculties, to use and interpret experience in his own way'). These
two features, I have suggested, make Mill's account more plausible
than some of his contemporary critics were disposed to allow.
However, in discussing the two features, one important factor has
been omitted.

Again and again, the text of *On Liberty* makes reference to the
importance of freedom in the interests of 'human advancement',
or 'progress', or the 'growth of civilisation'. Mill defends his
principle by urging that the spirit of liberty is 'the only unfailing
and permanent source of *improvement*', and he justifies it as being

in the interests of man '*as a progressive being*'. He tells us that 'where not the person's own character but the traditions or customs of other people are the rule of conduct, there is wanting . . . quite the chief ingredient of individual and social *progress*.' (My emphases. All references are to the chapter 'Of Individuality'.) Examples of this sort could be multiplied, but the important point here is that it is not autonomy (self-determination) *alone* which Mill favours. Rather, he favours autonomy as a source (indeed the only unfailing and permanent source) of individual improvement, societal progress and the growth of 'civilisation'. Not only *On Liberty*, but the whole of Mill's philosophy is infused with this belief in the possibility of moral progress. Much of his argument in *The Subjection of Women* depends upon it and, as we shall shortly see, *Utilitarianism* must also be interpreted by reference to it. Stephen Collini has summarised Mill's vision as follows;

'Mill projected his differences with the majority of his contemporaries into a reassuring historical dimension. Mankind were strung out in an enormous caravan, slowly and often unwillingly trudging across the sands of time, with the English governing classes, in particular, reluctant to move from their particularly favoured oasis . . . It is always an advantage to portray one's opponents as committed to defending a quite arbitrary stopping-place along the route of progress, and the argument had a particular resonance when addressed to an audience of nineteenth-century English liberals who regarded such moral improvement as chief amongst the glories of their age.' (Mill, 1984, p.xiii)

This image of the human race as a caravan progressing along the road of moral improvement is an indispensable yet, I shall argue, ultimately damning feature of Mill's liberal political theory.

Moral progress and its place in Mill's philosophy

In order fully to understand Mill's commitment to the possibility of moral improvement and progress we must range wider than the text of *On Liberty* itself. Referring to modern criticism of Mill, I noted that a recurring question is whether his 'simple principle' in

On Liberty is compatible with his utilitarianism, or whether it signals a departure from earlier, Benthamite, beliefs. Crudely, the difficulty is this: in *Utilitarianism*, Mill tells us that 'actions are right in proportion as they tend to promote happiness, wrong in proportion as they tend to promote pain or the reverse of happiness' (Mill, 1962, p.257). However, there is at least a superficial tension between this doctrine and the liberty principle, for the latter implies that individual sovereignty is more important than individual happiness, whereas the former states that there is only one criterion for deciding what is right – consideration of what will promote happiness. Thus, the simple principle of *On Liberty* tells us that a person 'cannot rightfully be compelled to do or forbear because . . . *it will make him happier*' (my emphasis). But according to *Utilitarianism* what is right *just is* what promotes happiness, and it would appear to follow from this that if compelling someone will make him happier, then he ought to be compelled.

The following examples indicate how the two principles peel apart: if I know of someone who is acting contrary to his best interests, I may wish to intervene and prevent him from behaving in this way. I may, for instance, want to stop one of my students entering into a marriage which I judge will be disastrously unhappy. And I may be right in my judgement about the way the marriage will turn out. Similarly, I may wish to deter my colleagues from eating too much white sugar, or refined flour, because I think that in the long run they will be healthier, and therefore happier, if they do not. And again, I may be right in my judgement. In both these cases the principle of utility stipulates that I ought to do what will promote happiness, and thus appears to sanction almost unlimited interference. However, the liberty principle explicitly forbids such interference – 'we cannot rightfully compel another person because it will make him happier' says Mill.

Whatever the superficial tensions between the two principles, Mill himself is unembarrassed. Immediately after stating the principle of liberty, he goes on to assert, 'I regard utility as the ultimate appeal on all ethical questions, *but it must be utility in the largest sense, grounded on the permanent interests of man as a progressive being*' (my emphasis). He sees the principle of liberty as perfectly compatible with the dictates of utilitarianism, provided only that utility is understood in this 'largest' sense. What, then, is the 'largest sense'? The answer to this question may be given by comparing Mill's utilitarianism with Bentham's utilitarianism, and by examining Mill's reasons for advocating a revision of the Benthamite conception.

In his essay on Bentham Mill draws attention to various defects in Bentham's moral philosophy. In particular, he says that for Bentham 'man is never recognised . . . as a being capable of pursuing spiritual perfection as an end; of desiring for its own sake the conformity of his own character to this standard of excellence' (Mill, 1962, p.100). Man is construed simply as a creature with wants and desires which must be satisfied, but there is no implication that there may be better or worse desires, nobler or baser wants.

Against this, Mill insists that morality consists of two parts: the regulation of outward action, and the individual's own training of himself, his own character, affection and will. In this department, he says, Bentham's system is a complete blank. Indeed, he goes further and suggests that even the regulation of outward actions will be imperfect and halting without consideration of excellence of character or perfectibility (pp.100–3). Briefly, what Mill is objecting to is Bentham's insistence that individual wants are simply to be taken as brute – to be satisfied wherever possible, but never improved, refined, or made more noble. By contrast, Mill insists that utilitarian morality – properly understood in 'the largest sense' – must also take into consideration the possibility of improving and refining individuals' desires. It must ask not only what men want, but what it is good that they should want. Here, then, in the essay on Bentham, we find an indication of the differences between the two conceptions of utilitarianism: where Bentham's account differs from Mill's favoured version it is in the failure of the former to make reference to that perfectibility of character essential to the latter.

References to moral progress and improvement are scattered throughout Mill's writings. For example, *Utilitarianism* contains reference to a now notorious distinction between higher and lower pleasures: mindful of the criticism that utilitarianism is the philosophy of swine, Mill urges that this criticism is well-founded only if we assume that the pleasures of men are indistinguishable from the pleasures of swine. This, he declares, is not so: it is, famously, 'better to be a human being dissatisfied than a pig satisfied; better to be Socrates dissatisfied than a fool satisfied.

And if the fool, or the pig, are of a different opinion, it is because they only know their own side of the question. The other party to the comparison knows both sides.' And he immediately goes on to warn that 'capacity for the nobler feelings is a very tender plant, easily killed not only by hostile influences, but by mere want of sustenance' (Mill, 1962, p.260). Here, the teleological implications of his account are clear: human nature may flourish if properly nurtured, but otherwise will wither away and die. Part of the purpose of moral philosophy – the part almost wholly ignored by Bentham – is to say something about the proper conditions for human flourishing and the development of excellence. We must not suppose that morality consists exclusively in the satisfaction of wants, for wants may be better or worse, higher or lower, and utilitarianism will indeed degenerate into the philosophy of swine if we forget that there is the possibility of moral progress and spiritual improvement.

Moreover, when we do examine the conditions necessary for moral progress and spiritual improvement, we find that chief amongst these is liberty. Liberty is, says Mill, 'the only unfailing and permanent source of human improvement.' Thus, the correct moral theory is utilitarianism, but utilitarianism is to be understood 'in the largest sense'. It does not consist in making no distinction between the desires people have, but in making a clear distinction between higher and lower, nobler and baser, and in generating the conditions necessary for the flourishing of the higher and nobler. In particular, in fostering and promoting individual liberty.

Mill's commitment to moral progress thus serves both to distinguish his utilitarianism from Benthamite utilitarianism and, ostensibly, to reconcile the principle of utility with the principle of liberty. However, the price of reconciliation is high. He claims that 'the only unfailing and permanent source of improvement is liberty . . . since by it there are as many possible independent centres of improvement as there are individuals', and this claim implies not only that freedom will promote autonomy, independence, and self-determination, but also that autonomy promotes (or is even constitutive of) moral improvement. Yet even if we admit that freedom is a necessary pre-condition for the development of autonomy, it is far from clear that autonomous choices will also be, in Mill's sense, morally better ones. If the connection between autonomy and moral improvement is a contingent connection, then it does not invariably hold: we ordinarily believe that people may autonomously choose what is morally inferior. But on the other hand, if autonomy is (partly) constitutive of moral improvement, then Mill appears to be advancing an account of autonomy which is ultimately circular: autonomous choices are *by definition* choices for the morally better. In the former case, freedom is good only in so far as it leads to improvement – and there is no guarantee that it will always do that. In the latter case, there is a guarantee that freedom will lead to improvement, but the guarantee is obtained by denying that morally inferior choices are autonomous at all. Either way, the conclusion is not one which liberals ought to be happy to espouse. For the first alternative renders freedom a merely instrumental good, whilst the second makes morally inferior choices by definition non-autonomous.

Mill escapes these illiberal implications in his own writings only by coupling a belief in moral progress with a high degree of optimism about human nature. This is most clearly seen in his views on population policy, where he predicts that, through freedom and education, people will gradually refine their feelings to a point where affinity of taste and intellect will replace sexual passion as the main impulse to marriage. Population policy will not be needed, he says, as people will come to see for themselves that abstinence is superior to sex, just as the wise man sees that poetry is superior to pushpin. In short, 'Mill simply takes it for granted most of the time that – at least in the long run and for the great majority of people – a policy of tolerance, encouragement of social variety and concerned, non-coercive intervention will trigger, not any arbitrary range of self-regarding desires, but a very specific desire; that for individual self-improvement' (Smith, 1984, p.197).

It is therefore Mill's optimism which underpins his conviction that freedom and moral progress will unfailingly march together. But where that optimism falters, as it sometimes does, the illiberal implications come tumbling out. Thus, in *The Subjection of Women* he declares

'What marriage may be in the case of two persons of cultivated faculties, identical in opinions and purposes, between whom there exists that best kind of equality, similarity of powers and capacities with reciprocal superiority in them – so that each can enjoy the luxury of looking up to the other, and can have alternately the pleasure of leading and being led in the path of development – I will not attempt to describe. To those who can conceive it, there is no need; to those who cannot, it would appear the dream of an enthusiast. But I maintain, with the profoundest conviction, that this, and this only, is the ideal of marriage; and that all opinions, customs, and institutions which favour any other notion of it, or turn the conceptions and aspirations connected with it into any other direction, by whatever pretences they may be coloured, are relics of primitive barbarism.' (Mill, 1983, p.177).

And elsewhere he remarks that, 'One of the deepest seated and most pervading evils in the human mind is the perversion of the imagination and feelings resulting from dwelling on the physical relation and its adjuncts' (Mill, 1973, p.123). These are problematic stances for Mill: if there is a correct ideal of marriage (as he clearly thinks there is), and if failure to embrace that ideal constitutes a pervading evil (as he clearly thinks it does), then why freedom? By his scathing and dismissive reference to 'barbarism' he appears to reject the possibility that people might freely and autonomously choose a path other than the path of emotional refinement and moral perfection. He insists that freedom is necessary for autonomy, and that autonomy leads to (or is even constitutive of) moral progress. Ideals of marriage other than his own are therefore rejected as 'barbarian'. They are, presumably, the ideal of non-autonomous agents. And now appeal to autonomy is circular and unhelpful, for 'acting autonomously' means nothing more nor less than acting in accordance with the ideals which Mill himself embraces.

The point of this discussion is not to pour scorn on Mill's justification of freedom and of toleration. There are wider and more important implications than the mere fact that Mill got it wrong. What I am suggesting here is that his philosophy is vitiated by his appeal to a conception of human nature which depends upon a doctrine of progress and perfectibility. Impressed by his own analogy between the individual and the tree which will grow and flourish if properly nurtured, Mill thinks that individuals too will flourish and become morally beautiful in a liberal environment. He never faces the possibility that they will use their freedom for less noble ends, nor does he seriously confront the fact that freedom for some may be freedom to enjoy pushpin, freedom to seek sexual gratification, or freedom to indulge the lower pleasures. When pressed, he is not all convinced that human beings are irreducibly diverse, and far more convinced that there is a single ideal of marriage, and a single correct attitude to sexuality.

At this point it is salutory to recall Mill's exclusion clause at the beginning of *On Liberty*. He explicitly excludes from his principle all those who have not reached the maturity of their faculties. But he now appears to be *defining* those who have reached the maturity of their faculties as those who do not, in fact, prefer pushpin to poetry, or sexual gratification to friendship. It appears that, on Mill's account, we declare our immaturity, our lack of autonomy, by our very decision to favour pushpin over poetry. And in so doing, we further declare our ineligibility to be protected by the liberty principle. The upshot is that Mill's optimism is the only thing which saves him from the deeply illiberal consequences of his own theory. And the point can be generalised: if liberalism seeks to justify its commitment to freedom and the toleration of diversity by a doctrine of autonomy, and if the doctrine of autonomy rests upon a belief in moral progress or perfectibility, then illiberal consequences will follow in all those cases in which freedom fails to promote the good.

Perhaps impressed by difficulties of this sort, modern writers in the liberal tradition, while accepting the spirit of Mill's liberalism, have renounced his attempt to justify it on the basis of a theory of human nature. In fact, it is a point of pride amongst many modern political philosophers that their theories involve no commitment to any theory of human nature or conception of the good life. Sandel expresses the point as follows:

'By virtue of its independence from ordinary psychological teleological assumptions, this liberalism, at least in contemporary versions, typically presents itself as immune from most controversies to which political theories have traditionally been vulnerable, especially questions of human nature and the meaning of the good life.' (Sandel, 1982, p.10)

Nevertheless, many such theories do rely upon a conception of autonomy as the basis of liberalism, and as a justification of liberalism's central values of freedom and toleration. What happens, therefore, in modern political theory is that commitment to autonomy, or self-determination, is retained, but it is retained in abstraction from the rich theory of human nature which forms its background and justification in Mill. To put the matter starkly, we might say that the concept of autonomy is stripped of Mill's optimism. It is by this manoeuvre that modern philosophers hope to retain Mill's valuable insights about the importance of freedom, diversity and toleration, while renouncing the unacceptable perfectibility thesis on which it is based. If this trick can be pulled off, then Mill's insight stands, and stands firmer than before, for once we have rid his theory of its perfectionist implications, we have also rid it of its illiberal implications. Liberalism will thus emerge purified, like the phoenix from the ashes.

It will be the aim of the next chapter to suggest that ultimately this argument cannot be made good and that modern liberalism, properly understood, inherits the defects of Mill's liberalism. My reasons for thinking that this is so are partly based upon the nineteenth-century objections to Mill's theory considered earlier. However, deeper than these specific points about the details of Mill's argument, is a further feature which has not yet been considered. In his biography of Mill, Michael St John Packe notes that *On Liberty* was published at a very unpropitious time: 'for better or worse, democracy was coming and the people knew it: the people, not the individual were to be the sovereign'. In Britain, in 1859, 'The tide was setting for Collectivism, and although there was profound disharmony about the form it was to take, all were agreed that man had no significance apart from the group or society of which he happened to be part . . . the era of the beehive state was dawning, and the freedom of the individual was going out of fashion' (Packe, 1954, pp.402–3).

Whether St John Packe is right about the collectivist atmosphere into which *On Liberty* was born, is a matter of historical judgement. Certainly, some commentators have doubted whether his analysis is entirely fair. But whatever the historical judgement, there is an important philosophical point here: Mill, and liberals following him, tend to defend liberty by means of organic and teleological analogies such as that of the Chinese lady's foot and of the tree flourishing 'according to the tendency of the inward forces which make it a living thing'. They emphasise the importance of allowing liberty to each to develop his own inherent nature, free from the constraints of society, and thus suggest that autonomy comes from within the individual. They concentrate on the extent to which the rules of society constrict individual freedom and autonomy, but in so doing they neglect the extent to which the rules of society may also form an essential background against which alone the development of freedom and autonomy is possible. Packe himself is an example of this. He says;

'Mill's doctrine of liberty may be incomplete, but it is more coherent than collectivism, which must seek refuge in the sophistry of the general will. Society is not an organism. When the finger is cut, the whole body bleeds; but when a man dies, unless he is heroic or ignoble, society at large is unaware. It is the individual, not the race, who sins or soars. It is the individual who is responsible.' (p.403)

All this is doubtless true, but even if it is the individual who is responsible, and the individual who is autonomous, it may still require appeal to the collective – to society at large – to explain how that autonomy is formed and developed. As we have seen, Mill gives some attention to this, but his remarks are almost wholly negative. He concentrates on the ways in which society may interfere with, restrict, and hinder the development of autonomy. He sees autonomy as coming from within, developing naturally from the inner nature of the individual. In his eyes, individual autonomy is to be contrasted with societal interference, but there are some respects in which individual autonomy is dependent upon societal interference, and this is a subject on which Mill remains almost totally silent.

In the next chapter, I shall suggest that the image of the Chinese lady's foot, the image employed so extensively by Mill, is an image which carries over into modern liberalism. This image, I shall argue, is defective, and the more so when (as in modern political philosophy) it is stripped of the theory of human nature with which it is associated in Mill. In order to make sense of the notion of autonomy on which liberalism is so often founded, we need not only the image of the Chinese lady's foot, but also the image of the beehive state. We need to understand how people are *inter*dependent as well as *in*dependent. We need to explain how autonomy is formed, not solely from the internal nature of individuals themselves, but also from the nature of the society in which they find themselves.

4 The Justification of Toleration

'The Brave, Naked Will'

There are three questions central to this book: 'What is toleration?', 'Why is it thought to be good?' and 'What are its limits?' In discussing the theories of Locke and Mill, some consideration has been given to each of these questions, and to the ways in which toleration has been understood in the history of political philosophy. However, the discussions so far have been historically selective in one very important sense: both Locke and Mill are writers squarely in the liberal tradition of political theory. Indeed, as we have already seen, Mill's defence of toleration is standardly regarded as *the* characteristically liberal defence; the argument from autonomy is 'sometimes thought to be the specifically liberal argument for toleration: the one argument which is not shared by non-liberals, and which displays the spirit of the liberal approach to politics' (Raz, 1988, p.155).

This liberal spirit is itself something which, it is claimed, leads naturally to the centrality of toleration: in the standard characterisations of political societies, liberal states are construed as open, diverse, plural, equally hospitable to all the beliefs and activities its members espouse, whereas socialist (particularly Marxist) societies are perceived as closed, monolithic, uniform. Far from welcoming diversity, they perceive it as deviance. If toleration consists in permitting and even welcoming diverse and sometimes disagreeable forms of behaviour, then toleration will be a central value of the liberal state, but not of a socialist state.

In this and the next chapter, I shall discuss the justifications of and limitations on toleration offered by modern political theorists

69

in the liberal tradition. Additionally, I shall discuss the harmonious connection which is often thought to exist between liberal political theory and the value of toleration. The aims here will be two-fold: firstly, to explain the precise nature and status of liberal commitment to toleration, and secondly to indicate how many of the difficulties inherent in historical liberalism (especially in Mill's account) carry over into modern accounts.

Briefly, my argument will be that liberalism needs a theory of human nature in order to obtain an adequate conceptual underpinning. However, once that theory of human nature is provided, illiberal implications follow from it: the precise theory of human nature which liberals adopt is a theory of human nature which has potentially illiberal consequences, particularly for those people or groups of people who are not themselves liberals. If this argument is correct, then the liberal claim to be particularly well-suited to assert and justify the value of toleration will be seriously undermined. The following chapter will argue that the claim *is* seriously undermined and that liberalism cannot deliver on its promise of a truly tolerant society: liberal justifications of toleration must either (surprisingly) give way to more socialist justifications, or they must construe toleration more narrowly than is usual in modern political philosophy – they must revert to a more pragmatic, Lockean conception of toleration.

What is liberalism?

The first problem, however, is to define liberalism itself. In a recent book, *Political Ideologies*, Robert Eccleshall describes modern liberalism as 'the liquorice allsorts of the political world, incorporating an assortment of good things in no coherent state of organisation' (Eccleshall, 1984, p.39), and in similar vein John Dunn refers to contemporary liberalism as 'an array of shreds and tatters of past ideological improvisation and highly intermittent current political illumination' (Dunn, 1985, p. 10).

These two quotations indicate the difficulty of explaining liberal justifications of toleration: to give a coherent account of liberalism's commitment to toleration presupposes a clear understanding of what liberalism itself is. Yet such a clear understanding is difficult to obtain. In earlier chapters, I have referred to Locke and Mill as archetypal liberals. I have spoken of the autonomy-based justification of toleration as *the* specifically liberal justification, and have generally implied that there is such a thing as a single, coherent, unified doctrine of liberalism, or at least an identifiable liberal tradition. At the same time, however, the contrast between Locke's account of toleration and Mill's account of toleration (both firmly within the liberal tradition) cast doubt upon this simple analysis. In almost every respect Locke and Mill differ in the justifications they offer. Mill bases almost his entire case on commitment to the values of diversity and individuality; Locke displays no such commitment. Mill argues fiercely for the moral wrong done by tyranny and oppression of all kinds; Locke simply thinks (religious) oppression to be irrational. Mill inveighs against social intolerance; Locke is exclusively concerned with its legal manifestations.

Difficulties of this sort are compounded when we turn from historical to modern liberalism. Philosophers as diverse as John Rawls, Robert Nozick and Ronald Dworkin are all classified as liberals, yet their justifications of liberalism and their accounts of what characterises it are dramatically different, as are their analyses of the character and structure of the liberal state. They advance different grounds for liberalism, and consequently advocate different limits of liberty. Thus, Robert Nozick construes compulsory taxation as an illegitimate infringement of individual liberty, and likens it to enforced labour (Nozick, 1974, pp.169– 72). John Rawls, however, has no such scruples, and his liberal state is essentially a redistributive or welfare state (Rawls, 1971). Similarly, writers who unite in describing themselves as 'liberals' may disagree violently as to the propriety of reverse discrimination, of laws against pornography, and laws requiring the use of seat belts in cars. Although they are all, in some sense, liberals they differ about the interpretation of 'liberty' in political contexts, and they also differ about the priority which should be accorded to liberty. How, then, are we to begin to formulate an account of liberalism?

The definition of liberalism

The entry on Liberalism in the *Encyclopaedia of Philosophy* tells us that 'by definition, a liberal is a person who believes in liberty'. But this definition, innocuous though it may appear, asserts both too much and too little. Too much, because there are some liberals who would deny even this: Ronald Dworkin, for example, insists that equality – not liberty – is the basic value of liberalism. On his view, liberals have no fundamental commitment to liberty, but only a commitment to those liberties which are necessary if we are to treat people as equals. Liberals do not value liberty *more* than they value equality, says Dworkin. Rather, they value liberty only *because* they value equality (Dworkin, 1985, chs 9, 10).

On the other hand, the definition also says too little, for in this simple form it masks the fact that 'liberty' may be variously interpreted. Isaiah Berlin's famous distinction between negative and positive conceptions of liberty illuminates this fact (Berlin, 1969, pp. 118–72). According to Berlin, negative liberty concerns the extent to which an agent may act unconstrained by obstruction or interference from others; 'I am normally said to be free to the degree to which no man or body of men interferes with my activity. Political liberty in this sense is simply the area within which a man can act unobstructed by others' (p.122). By contrast, positive liberty refers to the extent to which the agent is in control of his own life; 'the positive sense of the word "liberty" derives from the wish on the part of the individual to be his own master . . . I wish to be the instrument of my own, not other men's acts of will. I wish to be a subject, not an object; . . . a doer – deciding, not being decided for, self-directed and not acted upon by external nature or by other men as if I were a thing, or an animal, or a slave' (p.131).

On the negative conception of liberty an individual is free just in so far as no external obstacles prevent him from doing the thing he wishes to do. On the positive conception, however, this absence of external constraint is not the hallmark of freedom: genuine freedom requires that the agent be master of his own destiny, in control of his life and, arguably, in control of his own desires and preferences. Thus, the answer to the question 'Am I free?' will be determined, in large part, by the conception of freedom being employed. Moreover, the negative–positive distinction is far from exhaustive. Some have held conceptions of freedom which cut across the negative–positive divide, urging that the negative theorist is right to construe freedom as a matter of political organisation, but wrong to think that freedom increases as state intervention declines. Far from being defined as the ability to act unobstructed by the state and its laws, freedom consists in not construing those laws as obstructions at all (Cooper, 1983, p.131ff).

One final point: the characterisation of positive liberty is itself problematic. To describe a person as free in so far as he is self-directed is ambiguous. Does it mean simply that he is free if he does what he *actually* wants (if he acts on the desires he in fact has), or does it mean that he is free if he does what he *would* want if he were rational (if he acts on the desires he would have if he had perfect self-knowledge and rationality)? The former interpretation commits us to construing the drug addict and the alcoholic as free (since what they actually want is drugs or alcohol); the latter interpretation appears to open the door to unlimited interference in the name of freedom (it licences frustrating an individual's actual wants 'for his own good'). Commenting on this point, David Cooper writes;

'Isaiah Berlin has condemned the "monstrous impersonation" of equating what a man *would* choose (if he were more rational . . .) with what he *does* choose. But it is certainly intelligible to deny that a man really wants to do what it is his expressed desire to do . . . In an age that speaks easily of unconscious desires, of self-deception, of ideology and of bad faith, the idea has surely been abandoned (if it was ever there) that wants are transparent to their owners.' (1983, p.134)

Cooper's statement echoes Mill's belief that people numbed by the social pressure for conformity ultimately have no 'opinions or feelings of home growth or *properly* their own' (Mill, 1978, p.126). Of course, such people sincerely claim to believe and desire certain things, but these desires are not genuinely theirs. We are unfree to the extent that we are driven by desires which are not truly our own – either because they are the desires of other people, which we uncritically adopt, or because they are desires which express our self-deception and lack of knowledge. Here again, the answer to the question, 'Am I free?' will depend upon whether freedom is held to consist in satisfying the desires I actually have, or in satisfying the desires I would have if I were more rational, or better informed, or more self-willed, or more self-disciplined (Taylor, 1979, pp.175–93).

The upshot of all this is to indicate that the initial definition of liberals as people who believe in liberty, is inadequate; some say that it is straightforwardly false. Not all liberals do believe in liberty – at least, not in the sense that they take liberty to be *the* fundamental value of their liberalism. Moreover, even those who would concur with the definition, agree only in their use of the word, not about its meaning. As soon as questions are asked about what 'liberty' means, the apparent consensus disappears. As Jeremy Waldron has put it: 'To say that a commitment to *freedom* is the foundation of liberalism is to say something too vague and abstract to be helpful, while to say that liberals are committed fundamentally to a particular conception of liberty is to sound too assured, too dogmatic about a matter on which, with the best will in the world, even ideological bedfellows are likely to disagree' (Waldron, 1987, p.131).

The possibilities for liberalism

Against this background of dissent and confusion, can anything be done to isolate the theoretical foundations of liberalism? Some help can be gained by returning to its historical origins. In discussing historical theories of toleration several considerations crucial to liberalism have already surfaced. First, there is the alleged connection between intolerance and truth – the connection embodied in Bossuet's declaration, 'I have the right to persecute you because I am right and you are wrong.' Second, there is the connection between toleration and autonomy – the connection embodied in Mill's insistence on the importance of choosing one's own way of life. Third, there is the connection between toleration and specific reasons for interference – the connection expressed by Locke's argument that there is no right to freedom of worship as such, but only a right not to have one's worship interfered with for religious reasons.

In each of these cases, the argument for toleration is paralleled by an argument for liberalism. Thus, it has been claimed that liberalism is based on scepticism (the denial that there is such a thing as moral or religious truth); that it is based on autonomy;

and that it is based on a doctrine of neutrality with respect to reasons. These parallels are unsurprising since toleration is a central virtue of liberal societies, which are generally envisaged as societies in which people will practice and pursue a variety of opposing and incommensurable life styles.

> 'Some liberals celebrate the diversity of beliefs, commitments, ideals and life-styles held and practised in our community. Others accept simply as a matter of fact that that diversity is irreducible to a single orthodoxy, no matter how rationally compelling that orthodoxy may be. And others are convinced by Mill's arguments that any attempt to homogenize the ethical or religious life of our society would be ethically and socially disastrous.' (Waldron, 1987, p.144)

In any of these circumstances toleration will be regularly demanded, for it is in the nature of the case that some of the many and diverse life styles will be thought to be distasteful and even morally reprehensible. Liberalism thus begins from a premise of individual diversity: each person has his own unique conception of what makes life worth living and is entitled to pursue that conception to the best of his ability. If this is the guiding belief of liberalism, then the belief itself forces the need for toleration. Justifications of liberalism will, in part, be justifications of the toleration of that diversity which is valued by a liberal society. But how is this initial premise of liberalism to be converted into a justification of it? I shall discuss each of the three routes in turn.

Liberalism and scepticism

It is sometimes claimed that liberalism rests ultimately on moral scepticism. The thought here is that allowing freedom to individuals to pursue their different and competing lifestyles can best be justified on the assumption that there is nothing to choose between those life styles, or (slightly differently) that no one is in a position to choose. In his book *Social Justice in the Liberal State* Bruce Ackerman cites this as one of the 'main highways' to the liberal state. 'There are,' he says, 'no moral meanings hidden in the bowels of the universe. All there is is you and I struggling in a world that neither we nor any other thing created' (Ackerman, 1980, p.368). The implication is fairly clear: since there are no God-given truths about the best way to live, it is illegitimate for any individual or group to impose a way of life, or a set of values, upon another group. The liberal society, as a plural and tolerant society, is justified because no one is in a position to assert the superiority of his own values.

Ackerman's claim looks very like the reverse of Bossuet's claim, mentioned earlier: 'I have the right to persecute you because I am right and you are wrong.' Bossuet's intolerance was justified by his insistence that there was such a thing as truth and he was possessed of it: Ackerman's tolerance is justified by his insistence that there is no moral truth and therefore no one can properly presume to impose it. Scepticism entails pluralism, whereas objectivism entails intolerance.

However, before jumping too quickly to these conclusions, we should note two facts about the relationship between scepticism and toleration. Firstly, that as a matter of historical fact, scepticism has frequently been associated with persecution rather than with toleration. Secondly, that there are reasons for thinking that scepticism cannot provide a principled defence of toleration, but only a pragmatic one: it cannot tell us why toleration has moral value, but only, and at most, why it is sometimes a rational and expedient policy.

In a recent article on the historical foundations of toleration, Richard Tuck points out that seventeenth-century sceptics frequently coupled advocacy of scepticism with commitment to the life of *ataraxia* (imperturbability). This involved both detachment from the passions and detachment from moral and religious belief. The sceptical life was a life in which no belief was strongly held. It was a life of tranquillity, not a life of profound commitment or intense emotion. Sceptics of this persuasion were, however, confronted by the uncomfortable fact that many of those around them did not share their commitment to *ataraxia*. On the contrary, they took moral and religious beliefs very seriously indeed. To repress such people would be disingenuous of the sceptic, for it would indicate that he too took the beliefs seriously – seriously enough to oppose them publicly. On the other hand, to ignore them would be to risk civil strife, which would almost certainly destroy the very thing the sceptic prized most highly – the life of *ataraxia* itself.

Faced with this dilemma, sceptics insisted that moral principles be subordinated to political ones, and that toleration be countenanced only in circumstances where it would not generate the civil strife likely to threaten the life of *ataraxia*. Mindful of the fact that certain practices were likely to cause civil strife, sceptics frequently took the course of intolerance and persecution. The practical circumstances in which they found themselves dictated that toleration was inappropriate. Thus, in the history of the subject, both toleration and intolerance have been the practical consequences of moral and religious scepticism (Tuck, 1988, pp.21–35).

These historical facts about the connection between scepticism and toleration are paralleled by conceptual points about the relationship between scepticism and the liberal commitment to diversity. Whatever the apparent kinship between scepticism and liberalism, there is no entailment relationship between the two. Just as sceptics need not favour diversity, so those who favour diversity need not be sceptics. Liberals who are committed to the importance of a plural society may be so committed because (like Ackerman) they believe that there are no moral truths hidden in the bowels of the universe. They may think that there is no right way to live, but only ways preferred by different people, and this sceptical belief may lead them to favour toleration.

It may. But it need not. Commitment to pluralism may be underpinned by a firm belief that one way of life is best, yet modified by, for example, the equally firm belief that that way of life is valuable only if chosen freely. In other words, liberals may be committed to truth in moral matters, but nevertheless think that the value of truth is less than the value of allowing people to choose for themselves. As we have already seen, both Locke and Mill appealed to just such a thought in their arguments for toleration. We may recall Mill's claim that a person's 'own mode of laying out his existence is best, not because it is the best in itself, but because it is his own mode' (Mill, 1978, p.133). In saying this, Mill implies that there is a truth about the best way to lead one's life, but that it is better that people should find their own way to that truth than that the truth be imposed. Of course, part of the purpose of the earlier discussion of Mill was to suggest that he has a greater commitment to truth than he would have us believe: that his defence of freedom is premised upon an optimism which dictates that people will freely choose the right path. But such optimism is not invariably or necessarily associated with the commitment to freedom.

A further, very important, reason for rejecting the sceptical justification of liberalism is this: I have characterised liberal societies as having certain distinctive features – they are open, plural, diverse societies in which a wide variety of opposing and incommensurable ways of life may be pursued. Liberalism begins from a premise of individual diversity, and whatever justification of liberalism is offered in modern political theory, there is a high degree of consensus that the resulting liberal state will display these characteristics. But such a society, far from affirming no values (as scepticism requires), affirms the values of freedom and toleration. Liberty and toleration are part of the constitutive morality of liberalism, and it can hardly be open to liberals to defend these values on the sceptical ground that *no* values can be defended. In other words, if scepticism says that no set of values is better than any other, liberalism says at least this, that the values of freedom and toleration are better than the values of persecution and intolerance. So liberalism asserts what scepticism denies – that some values are superior to others. There are, therefore, three reasons for rejecting the attempt to justify liberalism by reference to moral scepticism:

1. The history of liberalism shows no clear connection between it and scepticism, nor does it show any connection between scepticism and toleration.
2. Liberalism (with its intrinsic commitment to diversity) does not entail a conceptual commitment to scepticism, nor vice versa.
3. Liberalism actually contains a commitment to the rejection of scepticism (at least in its cruder forms), since liberalism affirms what scepticism denies, namely that some values are objectively better than others – notably the values of freedom and toleration.

What, then, of the two other proposed justifications of liberalism? The claim that it is based upon neutrality and the claim that it is based upon autonomy? Again, we should note that these justifications share general assumptions about the characteristics of a liberal society – that it will be one in which freedom and toleration are valued, and where people with differing ideals and aspirations will live side by side.

Liberalism and neutrality

In his article 'Liberalism, Autonomy and the Politics of Neutral Concern' Joseph Raz refers to a liberal tradition 'which pins its defence of liberty on the adoption of some principles of political restraint' which are, in turn, 'manifestations of a politics of neutral concern' (Raz, 1982, pp.89–91). The guiding thought here is that (at least some) political actions should be neutral between competing conceptions of the good life. All societies will contain people of differing temperament, differing aspirations, differing religious beliefs, differing conceptions of the best way to live. The neutrality requirement is the requirement that such people should be allowed to lead their own lives in their own way (consistent, of course, with similar liberties for others), and that government should refrain from favouring any one group over another. Thus the refusal, in America, to establish any one church is held to be evidence of political neutrality between members of different sects. Raz claims that 'when principles of neutral political concern are used to provide the foundation of a political theory, they can be regarded as attempts to capture the core sense of the liberal ethos' (p.91).

The liberal ethos, as here identified, is one which takes as given the fact that people have certain desires and preferences and that those desires and preferences may differ one from another. It is illegitimate for government to favour one set of preferences over another, or to discriminate against a particular set of preferences. As Brian Barry has put the matter:

'Classical liberalism had other strands than this one, no doubt, but one was certainly the idea that the state is an instrument for satisfying the wants that men happen to have rather than a means of making good men (i.e. cultivating desirable wants or dispositions in its citizens)' (Barry, 1965, p.66)

In brief, government must be neutral as between competing conceptions of the good. It is not the role of the state to dictate a way of life for its citizens. Government has only the role of facilitating whichever ways of life already seem good to people. Here, in very simple form, is the liberal ethos which, it is claimed, serves to justify liberalism's commitment to liberty. It will be my argument here that this justification is ultimately vacuous. However, before explaining why that is so, it is worth looking at some familiar, but I think unconvincing criticisms of the neutrality principle.

Criticisms of neutrality

One objection commonly raised is that allegiance to neutrality will collapse into moral scepticism, and that since scepticism will not do as a foundation for liberalism, neither will neutrality. Ronald Dworkin makes exactly this complaint. He says, 'Liberalism based on neutrality finds its most natural defence in some form of moral scepticism, and this makes it vulnerable to the charge that liberalism is a negative theory for uncommitted people' (Dworkin, 1985, p.205). He takes the example of liberal opposition to government intervention on matters of sexuality and insists that this cannot be explained by reference to scepticism. In such a case, he argues, 'scepticism seems exactly the wrong answer to make, because if the moral majority is wrong, and each person should be free to choose personal ideals for himself, then this is surely because the choice of one sort of life over another is a matter of supreme importance, not because it is of no importance at all' (Dworkin, 1983, p.47).

Dworkin's account of liberalism based upon sceptical neutrality recalls the seventeenth-century scepticism mentioned in the previous section. He implies that the sceptic will renounce all commitment to the importance of moral judgements, and will adopt an air of detached indifference where moral matters are concerned. However, two questions arise here: firstly, is it true that neutrality must collapse into scepticism? (Is the neutralist inevitably commited to being a sceptic?) Secondly, must scepticism take quite this seventeenth-century form (must the sceptic eschew the importance of moral and religious belief)?

The first question can be dealt with quite briefly. We have already seen that the guiding belief which leads to the requirement of neutrality is the belief in individual diversity – the belief that each person has his own conception of what makes life worth living and is entitled to pursue that conception to the best of his ability. But scepticism need not follow from this: we may think *both* that human nature is diverse *and* that there are right answers to questions about the good life. Of course, given the diversity of human nature, there need be no single right answer (no single way in which everyone should live). There will, nevertheless, be better or worse alternatives for each individual. To draw a trivial analogy, I may believe that people exhibit diversity in physical size: that there is no one shirt size which is suitable for all people. Nevertheless, it does not follow that there is no right answer to the question 'What is the best shirt size for me?' Obviously, the analogy is partial and imperfect, but all it is meant to indicate is that the fact of diversity does not entail that there are no right answers.

Relatedly, belief in neutrality may be underpinned not by scepticism but by belief in the value of autonomy. I may think that there is a right way for each person to live, and I may even think that there is one single way of life which is best for all people. Yet this belief can be outweighed by the belief that it is better for people to choose their own way of life than to have a way of life imposed on them.

In the previous section I argued that, superficial appearances notwithstanding, there is no entailment relationship between scepticism and liberalism. Similarly, there is no entailment between the neutrality thesis and scepticism. A proponent of neutrality is not thereby committed to scepticism, though it may be true, as Dworkin claims, that 'the neutrality thesis makes liberalism much more vulnerable to the familiar charge that it is based on moral scepticism or nihilism' (Dworkin, 1983, p.47).

What, then, of the second question, 'Are sceptics committed to denying the importance of moral judgements?' At this point, I want to backtrack a little on the argument of the section on scepticism. There I suggested not only that scepticism does not entail liberalism, but that liberals must not be sceptics – the liberal commitment to values of freedom and toleration carries with it a rejection of any sceptical thesis which insists that there are no values. However, it is important not to rest content with this conclusion, but to inspect rather more closely exactly what scepticism amounts to. In the earlier section I implied that sceptics are simply and straightforwardly committed to the notion that, since there are no moral truths, it does not matter what values we espouse, nor how we choose to lead our lives. Certainly, Dworkin implies that this is how he understands scepticism: 'scepticism seems exactly the wrong answer to make . . . because the choice of one sort of life over another is a matter of supreme importance, not a matter of no importance at all' (ibid.). This, however, is a crude and extreme form of scepticism. Not all sceptics make the move from thinking that there is no right answer to thinking that it does not matter how we choose. Questions of truth are separate and distinguishable from questions of importance.

Consider the following example: some years ago a panel of experts was asked to choose the twenty five best post-war novels. Their choice was greeted by howls of rage from, amongst others, Mr Anthony Burgess, who promptly published his own list of best novels. In the Introduction to that list he makes it clear that he thinks both that there is no definitive or right list, and that the choice is an important one. 'There are no universal laws', he says, 'but *Anna Karenina* is a great novel and *The Carpetbaggers* an inferior one' (Burgess, 1984, p.20). Scepticism need not degenerate into an extreme relativism according to which everything is a matter of opinion and any opinion is as good as any other, nor need it commit us to thinking that anything goes and that nothing is important. *Pace* Dworkin, I may think that some choices are important ones, even though I believe that there is no single right choice.

The following conclusions may therefore be drawn from this discussion:

1. Some neutralists (like Ackerman) may be happy with scepticism.
2. Even if they are sceptical, they need not be committed to the belief that choices are important only in those areas where truth is attainable.
3. They need not, in any case, base their neutrality thesis on scepticism. They can, instead, base it on autonomy.

To say this much, however, is simply to note some things to which the neutralist need not be committed. It is not to say exactly what neutrality actually consists in, nor whether it offers an adequate justification of liberalism. I turn now, therefore, to these issues.

The nature of neutrality

Earlier in the chapter I referred to the neutrality requirement as one which demands official government neutrality on questions of the good life. The lack of an established church in America was cited as one way in which a liberal society preserves its neutrality. But is it true that, by having no established church, American society is officially neutral? To answer this question we must look more closely at what neutrality consists in.

Broadly speaking, there are two ways in which the neutrality requirement might present itself: some philosophers have insisted on neutrality with respect to reasons for state action, while others have concentrated on neutrality with respect to the outcome of state action. Thus Locke, for example, falls into the former camp, since his argument for religious toleration requires only that the state should not intervene against religious practices for purely religious reasons. By contrast, Lord Scarman appears to favour the latter approach, for he argues that the consequences of laws should not be such as to discriminate against a particular group. He urges that Muslims should have the same opportunity to attend the mosque as Catholics have to attend Mass. Each conception of neutrality has its own inherent difficulties. If we require neutrality with respect to reasons, then it may appear that the presence of neutrality can be ascertained only by inspecting the inner motivation of legislators, and this is a notoriously difficult task and one which invites sophistry. Moreover, it is far from clear that neutrality with respect to reasons, even if applied without sophistry, will always dictate policies which are tolerant: where a government is highly concerned (or obsessive) about matters of security, its policies may well be extremely restrictive and illiberal, even though they are (officially) neutral. For example, a government with sincere but unfounded fears about its own ability to exercise authority might outlaw certain religious practices. The government might sincerely believe that such practices posed a threat to civil order and peace in society. In these circumstances, their policy would be officially neutral. It would, nevertheless, be highly intolerant. Thus, restricting neutrality to reasons for action is not, in itself, a guarantee of liberal political practice. By the same token, however, demanding neutrality with respect to consequences is far from straightforward: on a practical level, it is often very difficult to predict what the consequences of a piece of legislation will be, and even if that were possible, the demand for neutrality in this sense presupposes a clear and uncontroversial criterion for determining when a piece of legislation actually is neutral in its effects.

That these two interpretations of the neutrality requirement may deliver different answers to the same question can be seen by considering laws governing Sunday trading. At present, the law of England and Wales imposes stringent restrictions on what may be bought and sold on a Sunday. Would government be acting neutrally if it were to revise these laws so as to allow unrestricted Sunday trading? If we take the reason-based notion of neutrality and couple it with the assumption that such a revision would not be introduced simply in order to make life difficult for practising Christians, then we must conclude that the new law would be neutral. However, if we take the consequences-based notion of neutrality, then such a law certainly would not be neutral, for its predictable (though not its intended) effect would be to discriminate against practising Christians by making it more difficult for them to trade competitively.

Moreover, once we adopt this consequences-based account of neutrality, it becomes doubtful whether any law could in principle be neutral as between competing conceptions of the good. In this particular case, to have no restriction on Sunday trading is to favour the atheist or the non-Christian over the Christian. But to have *some* law governing Sunday trading is to favour the Christian. Therefore, whether we have some law or no law, we are failing (in this sense) to be neutral between competing conceptions of the good.

A related question, and one which has already been alluded to in discussing Lord Scarman's claim, is how minimalist neutrality is meant to be. Are governments neutral if they simply do not forbid certain practices, or is it required that they should give equal aid to all practices? In his 1983 Morrell Address Lord Scarman cites the case of the Muslim schoolteacher who wished to take Fridays off from school in order that he might attend the mosque. His headmaster refused permission for this, and the teacher complained that the rule (and the law) were non-neutral. 'The Muslim said that the Jews were all right; they have Saturday. The Christians are all right, they have Sunday, why should he not have his holy day on Friday' (Scarman, 1987, p.55). Does neutrality require simply that there be no law forbidding attendance at mosque on Friday, or does it require more than that? Does it require positive aid and assistance to members of the Muslim faith, who (unlike Christians) face a stark choice between practising their religion and fulfilling their professional commitments?

If, like Scarman, we favour the latter, then we must accept that this conception of neutrality may have extensive resource implications in some cases. For example, the requirement of neutrality in outcome might involve huge expense in the case of some minority groups. 'It may well be that in the absence of positive support from the state certain minority ways of life will be eroded. This is often true in the case of minority language groups. By doing nothing to promote bilingualism, the state may allow the demise of a minority language, so that for example the Welsh language, in the absence of positive policies, would go the way of Cornish. To prevent this happening, the state will have to undertake positive policies ranging from provision of teaching resources through to support for the media in, say, the form of a special television channel' (Weale, 1985, pp.27–8).

Examples of this sort of problem can be multiplied, but the central point is that the bare assertion of neutrality is profoundly ambiguous – even vacuous – unless it is accompanied by an account of why exactly neutrality is important. We cannot know what the neutrality requirement amounts to, nor what it demands of us in practice unless we are able to give an account of its conceptual justification. In the remainder of this section, I shall suggest that the reason liberals favour neutrality is because (like Mill) they favour an autonomy-based conception of liberalism. It is the notion of autonomy which will provide content for the neutrality requirement and which will explain why and in what sense liberals favour neutrality.

Why liberals favour neutrality

Throughout this chapter, emphasis has been placed on the differences which divide modern liberals. The central premise of liberalism – the premise of individual diversity – generates a variety of different approaches to the problem of justifying liberalism, and much of the discussion so far has concentrated on the different kinds of justification which may be offered for liberalism in modern political theory. Appeal to scepticism and appeal to the doctrine of neutrality are just two possibilities. However, emphasis on the differences which divide modern liberals ought not to mask the similarities which unite. One important feature of modern liberalism is its insistence that it does not subscribe to any particular view of human nature. As Sandel puts it, 'liberalism, in its contemporary versions, typically presents itself as immune to most controversies to which political theories have traditionally been vulnerable, especially questions of human nature and the meaning of the good life' (Sandel, 1982, p.10). One of the difficulties with Mill's liberalism, and with his defence of toleration, was precisely that, on inspection, it appeared far less liberal and far less tolerant than it initially claimed to be. The reason for this, I suggested, is that Mill is committed to a particular view of human nature. Whatever claims he may make about the importance of diversity, individuality and eccentricity, he nevertheless underpins this commitment to diversity by a doctrine of moral improvement and progress which incorporates a distinct view of what constitutes human good. It is this facet of his account which generates its illiberal implications.

Mindful of the fact that theories of human nature and doctrines of perfectibility may generate problems for liberalism, modern liberals have firmly rejected any such accounts and have prided themselves upon their refusal to make any connection between the political values they advocate (values of liberty and toleration) and an underlying theory of human motivation. Thus Rawls insists that his theory of justice depends upon 'no particular theory of human motivation'; Dworkin declares that his liberalism 'does not rest on any special theory of human personality'; and Ackerman states that liberals are not committed on any 'Big Questions' of epistemology and metaphysics (Rawls, 1971; Dworkin, 1985; Ackerman, 1980). These claims appear sensible: in so far as Mill's liberal credentials were undermined precisely by his commitment to perfectionist principles, modern liberalism does well to reject those principles and to remain agnostic about questions of human nature and the good for man. Indeed, it would appear that attempts to secure and justify neutrality will be seriously undermined once an assumption is made that there is such a thing as 'the good for man'.

Modern liberalism is thus underpinned by the denial of a strong form of perfectionism – the denial that there is any one way in which it is best to live. Against this background, the requirement of neutrality (whatever its specific interpretation) is the requirement that governments should 'let a thousand flowers bloom'. However, this claim, like the claim to base liberalism on scepticism, is somewhat Janus-faced: in order for governments to be neutral between competing conceptions of the good, there must be distinct and competing conceptions of the good. But some of those conceptions might include, as part of their morality, the belief that neutrality is fundamentally mistaken. Some people may believe that their own way of life is intrinsically superior to all others, and may be prepared – may even feel themselves morally obliged – to impose that way of life. In other words, the ways of life between which liberalism refuses to adjudicate may themselves be ways of life which insist that adjudication, and even imposition, is politically necessary.

The upshot of this is to place the neutralist in a serious dilemma: the *need* for neutrality is created by the fact of diversity, yet the *application* of neutrality is possible only on the assumption that diversity is underpinned by unity – at least about the propriety of the neutrality principle itself. What grounds are there, however, for thinking that people of widely differing moral and religious perspectives will nevertheless agree that the principle of neutrality is itself acceptable? (See Weale, 1985.)

One important feature of this problem is that it implies that liberalism does, after all, subscribe to a view of human nature and the good for man. In general, it implies that it is better for people to pursue their own way of life than for them to have a way of life thrust upon them. In particular, it implies the centrality of the value of autonomy in the liberal scheme of things. As indicated above, this need not amount to moral scepticism – to the belief that there is no right way to live. It will, however, imply at least this – that a way of life which is determined by individuals themselves is preferable to a way of life which is externally imposed.

This characteristic of liberalism is found not only in modern accounts, but also in the history of the theory: both Locke and Mill, divided though they are in their justifications of toleration, unite in the belief that ways of life, or conceptions of the good, which are forcibly imposed are valueless. This is at least part of Locke's claim when he insists that 'the care of each man's soul belongs to himself'. And it is similarly crucial to Mill's assertion that 'the way of life is best not because it is best in itself, but because it is chosen.' This notion of choice and its importance to the liberal conception, brings us to the third way of justifying liberalism – the justification in terms of autonomy.

In the remainder of this chapter, I shall discuss historical and contemporary justifications of liberalism and of toleration in terms of autonomy. My claim will be that this is the best explanation of liberalism's commitment to toleration. At the same time, however, this justification undermines liberalism's pretence to provide a theory which is divorced from conceptions of human nature and theories of the good for man.

Liberalism and autonomy

In discussing Mill's *On Liberty* I noted that 'autonomy' is not a term which Mill himself employs, but suggested that we might nevertheless gloss his defence of liberty in terms of a concept of autonomy as self-determination, or self-government. There are, however, two problems inherent in such a gloss. Firstly, the precise content of autonomy is inadequately explained (What exactly does self-determination consist in?). Secondly, and relatedly, it is simply assumed that the concept *can* be abstracted from the account of human nature with which it has traditionally been associated.

The aim of this section is to examine these problems in greater detail and also to look more closely at the three defining features of autonomy mentioned in the earlier chapter. These are, firstly, that the autonomous agent must be in a position to act – he must not be compelled by external forces or the threat of punishment (he must have negative freedoms). Secondly, that his actions must be performed in obedience to a law – he must not be pathologically driven by desires or impelled by irresistible urges which are such as to undermine his rationality. (He must be a *rational free chooser*.) Thirdly, that he must himself create or prescribe the law to which he is obedient. (He must be independent both of the coercive action and of the will of others.) These three constituent parts of the concept of autonomy – freedom, rationality and self-determination – must all be explained more fully if autonomy-based liberalism is to be vindicated. I begin, however, by looking at the concept of autonomy as it has featured in historical defences of liberalism.

What is autonomy?

As has been noted already, the concept of autonomy is most frequently associated with the writings of the German Enlightenment philosopher, Immanuel Kant. For Kant, autonomy is a property of the will, and the will is autonomous when it is not motivated by anything outside itself (by desires, inclinations, or the dictates of others). Autonomous agents are obedient to a law they have made for themselves. They are all and only rational beings or, in the Kantian jargon 'the will is conceived as a power of determining oneself to action in accordance with the idea of certain laws. And such a power can be found only in rational beings' (Kant, 1966, p.91).

The contrast which Kant is drawing here is, in part, a contrast between behaviour which is determined by outside influences and behaviour which comes from within the agent. Thus, for example, animals are determined in their behaviour by external causes: the dog sees a rabbit and instinctively pursues it. Its behaviour is non-autonomous because externally governed. Likewise, human beings may fail to be autonomous, either because (like the dog) they are influenced to action by external causes, or because they are driven by their own inner desires, and not by their rational will. Thus, the drug addict may be said to be non-autonomous because he is at the mercy of his own desire for drugs: he is the servant and not the master of his desires, and that he is so may be apparent to him as well as to us. Acting autonomously involves being free both from external constraint and from the tyranny of internal, yet irrational, desires. It involves being self-determined, where self-determination is a function of *reason*, not of desire. Why should this notion of autonomy as rational self-determination not simply be carried over into modern liberal theory?

One reason is that the above account omits to mention that Kant's claims about autonomy are the conclusions of a robust and somewhat unpalatable metaphysical argument according to which the autonomous will exists timelessly in a noumenal realm. In the 'Analytic' of the *Critique of Pure Reason* Kant insists that everything in the phenomenal realm (in the world as we know it) is causally determined (Kant, 1968). It follows from this that if there is to be human freedom and moral accountability, this must spring from something outside the phenomenal realm. The will which is free (the autonomous will) acts upon yet is distinct from and outside of the phenomenal realm.

This two-world view, unpalatable and abstruse as it may be, is crucial to the internal consistency of Kant's account. It is not, for him, an optional extra which we might abandon whilst holding on to the notion of autonomy as rational self-determination, for without the two-world view rational self-determination is impossible in Kant's eyes. He makes this clear in his essay 'What is Orientation in Thinking?', where he takes to task those romantics who would construe the concrete, personal, historically specific individual as the source of law. In doing this, Kant says, they abandon rationality entirely and replace it by mere feeling, contingency and history. The time-bound individual cannot be the source of *law* and that he cannot be the source of law is a matter of the first importance for Kant's conceptual scheme.

Kant construes the attempts of his critics to undermine the two-world view as attacks on reason itself, since for him the only place for reason is in a separate, noumenal realm. Therefore, denying the noumenal realm is denying reason: 'Men of intellectual power and broad minds! I honour your talents and your feeling for humanity. But have you considered what you do, and where you will end with your attacks on reason?', Kant asks (1949, p.303). And he makes it quite clear that without two distinct realms – the phenomenal and the noumenal – there could be no room for morality at all.

Nevertheless, it might be pointed out that the concept of autonomy has been instructively employed by many philosophers who do not share Kant's metaphysical presuppositions. So even if Kant is unable to give a coherent account of autonomy without the two-world view, it need not follow that nothing can be made of the idea of autonomy. However, when we turn from Kant to Locke and Mill, we find that the situation is not significantly different: if autonomy is understood as rational self-determination, then both Locke and Mill, when they appeal to the concept of autonomy, appeal to it against a particular background. Most importantly, their views of what counts as rational are determined by the teleological assumptions of their philosophy generally. They have very precise views about human nature which dictate what rationality consists in. Without these views it is questionable whether anything can be made of the notion of rationality at all. Yet it is precisely this which needs to be clarified and explained if modern accounts of autonomy as rational self-determination are to do any honest work.

In *Ethica* Locke writes 'A dependent, intelligent being is under the power of and direction and dominion of him on whom he depends and must be for the ends appointed him by that superior being. If man were independent he could have no law but his own will, no end but himself. He would be a god to himself and the satisfaction of his own will the sole measure of all his actions' (*Ethica* B, p.141, as quoted in Dunn, 1969, frontispiece). Locke's message is closely akin to Kant's: ordinary, time-bound individuals cannot act rationally. Where Kant appeals to metaphysics to provide the necessary background for his concept of rationality, Locke appeals to God. Of course, for Kant any such appeal to God would turn autonomous action into heteronomous action: the agent whose action is determined by something outside himself is non-autonomous, and it does not matter whether the outside influence is another person, or God. Nevertheless, the underlying point is the same in both writers – an explanation of properly autonomous action (action which is rational and self-determined) requires more than reference to the desires of the agent. Autonomy does not consist simply in doing what one wants: it consists in acting rationally, and we need a background against which to decide what counts as rational behaviour.

In a not dissimilar manner, Mill appeals implicitly to a teleological account of human nature to justify his claims about what is rational. In *Utilitarianism*, and in 'Bentham' he makes it perfectly

clear that he believes there to be rational ways of acting, *given* a
particular conception of human flourishing and the good for man.
His assessment of Bentham's philosophy is that it fails in the
consideration of the greater social questions, which, he says, 'must
be viewed as the great instruments of forming the national
character; of carrying forward the members of the community
towards perfection, or preserving them from degeneracy' (Mill,
1962). And here, as has already been argued, Mill has in mind
some notion of human perfection distinct from what men simply
happen to want. Although rejecting the theological underpinning
of Locke's account, Mill equally cannot accept that it is enough
for man's own desire to be the sole measure of all his actions.

The point of this brief foray into the history of liberalism is
simply to indicate that in each of the cases considered the notion
of autonomy as rational self-determination is explained either by
a robust metaphysics (as in Kant), or by a belief in the God of
Christianity (as in Locke), or by a doctrine of human nature and
perfectibility (as in Mill). In all these cases, what is rational is
dictated by the background assumptions. There is no notion here
of 'pure' rationality, but only of rationality *given* that God has
purposes for us, that there are recognised and uncontroversial
means of human flourishing, and so on. Against these backgrounds
certain things truly are irrational – denials of our own true nature,
or rejections of God's purpose for us. Yet it is precisely these sorts
of background which contemporary liberalism prides itself on
rejecting. 'This liberalism presents itself as immune from most
controversies to which political theories have traditionally been
vulnerable, especially questions of human nature and the meaning
of the good life' (Sandel, 1982, p.10).

The upshot of the above discussion is to cast doubt upon the
modern notion of autonomy, for what is indicated here is that
autonomy as *rational* self-determination needs background
assumptions to make it plausible. In the absence of these, the
notion of rationality is vacuous and the consequent concept of
autonomy too thin to do any work for us. Liberals therefore need
background assumptions about human nature in order to flesh out
the notion of autonomy. Those assumptions must be rich enough
to generate a non-vacuous concept of rationality, but at the same
time, they must not be so rich as to constitute a potentially
misleading account of human nature.

At this point it is sometimes suggested that there is a mistake inherent in construing autonomy as rational self-determination at all. What is required for autonomy is simply that people are governed by their own desires, not by the desires or wishes of others. This suggestion takes us back to the distinction between negative and positive liberty advanced by Berlin. In distinguishing between the two concepts of liberty, Berlin remarks upon the close connection between autonomy and theories of positive liberty:

> 'the "positive" conception of freedom as self-mastery, with its suggestion of a man divided against himself, has, in fact, and as a matter of history, of doctrine and of practice, lent itself more easily to this splitting of personality into two: the transcendent, dominant controller, and the empirical bundle of desires and passions to be disciplined and brought to heel.' (Berlin, 1969, p.134)

He inveighs against this interpretation, arguing that, far from being liberal, it is a recipe for tyranny and suppression. Once freedom is interpreted as rational self-mastery, once the foundation of liberalism is held to be autonomy in this sense, then the door is open for all kinds of illiberal acts in the name of liberalism itself. He remarks:

> 'once I take this view I am in a position to ignore the actual wishes of men and societies, to bully, oppress, torture them in the name, and on behalf, of their "real" selves, in the secure knowledge that whatever is the true goal of man (happiness, performance of duty, wisdom, a just society, self-fulfilment) must be identical with his freedom – the free choice of his "true", albeit often submerged and inarticulate self.' (Berlin, 1969, p.133)

And so it may be with autonomy: if the foundation of liberalism is autonomy, and autonomy is interpreted as rational self-determination, then we need to be vigilant. Just as Mill insisted that the principle of liberty applies only to those who have reached 'the maturity of their faculties', so autonomy-based liberalism generally implies that liberal principles are to be granted only to those who are autonomous. Moreover, unlimited interference may be justified in the name of the promotion of autonomy – as Berlin puts it, in the interests of the 'true' or 'real' or autonomous self, and in disregard of the actual desires of the empirical self.

Clearly there are dangers here, and we have already seen some of them in our discussion of Mill. However, it is far from obvious that all difficulties are removed if we renounce the notion of autonomy as rational self-determination. In particular, the attempt to derive liberalism simply from reflection on what people actually want is not a promising strategy:

> 'A man's freedom can be hemmed in by internal, motivational obstacles, as well as external ones. A man who is driven by spite to jeopardise his most important relationships, in spite of himself, as it were, or who is prevented by unreasoning fear from taking up the career he truly wants, is not really made more free if one lifts the external obstacles to his venting his spite or acting on his fear. Or at best he is liberated into a very impoverished freedom.' (Taylor, 1979, pp.191–2)

No more can such a man be said to be autonomous.

The difficulties with the concept of autonomy are therefore three-fold. Where autonomy is understood as rational self-determination, and rational self-determination is described by reference to a conception of human nature, then autonomy-based defences of liberalism fail to be liberal. They tend to degenerate into repressive and illiberal doctrines in the way described by Berlin. However, if the notion of rationality is given up and autonomy is described simply in terms of what men happen to want, then no sense can be made of the (commonplace) claim that people are often victims of their own desires. If autonomy is self-mastery, then self-mastery does not always consist in doing what I want, since I may sometimes be (and know myself to be) the victim and not the master of my own desires. Finally, and most importantly for our purposes, if autonomy is understood as rational self-determination, but without any background account of human nature, we may find difficulty in explaining when and why an action counts as rational at all. The content of rationality can be explained only via an explanatory background, so if modern liberalism renounces this background, it renounces the possibility of giving criteria for rationality.

The conclusion of this section, therefore, concerns the second of the two conditions for autonomy – that autonomy involves rational self-determination. What I am suggesting is that the modern liberal both needs and cannot have this condition as a constituent feature of autonomy. It is necessary in order to distinguish cases in which the agent is victim and not master of his desires. Yet it is illegitimate without a background story which provides criteria for rationality. Moreover, where that background is provided, autonomy often justifies illiberal acts in the name of liberalism itself.

Reflecting on modern liberalism's attempt to hold on to the concept of autonomy, but to deny theories of human nature, Iris Murdoch remarks, 'We no longer see man against a background of values, of realities, which transcend him. We picture man as a brave, naked will. We have bought the liberal theory as it stands . . . at the cost of surrendering the background' (Murdoch, 1961, p.18). In each of the examples considered here – the examples of Kant, of Locke, and of Mill – the metaphysical or teleological background is essential and the mistake of modern liberalism is to favour the doctrine of autonomy, of rational self-determination, without favouring the backgrounds which made those doctrines intelligible ones. This, as we shall shortly see, has serious consequences for liberalism's promise to deliver a truly diverse, plural and tolerant society.

The development of autonomy

Murdoch's reference to the modern liberal agent as a 'brave, naked will' introduces a further difficulty with modern autonomy-based liberalism. This is a difficulty generated by the third defining feature of autonomy – that the autonomous agent must be obedient to a law which he has created or prescribed for himself. This has been expressed as the requirement that he be 'part creator of his own world' (Raz, 1982, p.111), or that he 'distance himself in some measure from the conventions of his social environment and from the influences of those surrounding him' (Gray, 1983, p.74). What is encapsulated in these remarks is the demand that the autonomous agent be one who reflects upon and critically evaluates the standards and norms of his society. The notion of distance is therefore central to the characterisation of autonomy. However, it has also been problematic, for when taken to its limit it implies that such a thing as complete autonomy can be attained and that such autonomy consists in being completely detached from one's moral and social environment.

Such an idea has very little to recommend it and has rightly been rejected as involving an unrealistic neglect of the inherently social nature of man. It is generally agreed that the ideal of a completely free chooser is an unattainable fantasy. One reason for this is that autonomy is something which must be learned, and such learning requires that there be a background of shared values against which free and autonomous choices may be made.

A second reason is that autonomy is something which, once learned, must be sustained, and again this requires that there be not simply self-construction, but a background of values against which such construction can take place. The autonomous agent will indeed be a rational free chooser, but his autonomous choices must be made on the basis of reasons, and only appeal to such things as the social nature of man can provide the framework within which reasons will operate. Joseph Raz puts the matter this way, 'The completely autonomous person is an impossibility. The ideal of the perfect existentialist with no fixed biological and social nature who creates himself as he goes along is an incoherent dream' (Raz, 1982, p.112). Thus, the condition of autonomy requires distance from the world – being autonomous involves being detached from and in control of one's environment. At the same time, however, the development of autonomy requires proximity to the world – it requires that the agent learn and develop his autonomy within an environment and against a background supportive of that ideal.

This need for the agent to be both detached from yet embedded in his world is normally conceded by modern liberals, who then go on to behave as though there is nothing problematic about it: it is true that autonomy is something which we must learn within our world, and which is circumscribed by our world. This is why there can never be total or complete autonomy. However, it does not follow from that, the argument goes, that autonomy-based liberalism cannot be made internally consistent. What I want to concentrate on here is precisely the contention that all these strands of liberalism can be rendered compatible with one another.

In particular, I shall concentrate on the claims that:

1. The condition of autonomy requires distance from the world.
2. The development of autonomy requires proximity to the world.
3. Autonomy can only ever be partial, never complete.

My argument will be that although all these are central premises of autonomy-based liberalism, they nevertheless conflict in such a way as to undermine both the commitment to a maximally liberal society and the commitment to pluralism and tolerance. Although liberalism begins from the premise of individual diversity, and insists that each person is entitled to pursue his own conception of the good, that line of argument will be severely compromised once we analyse the precise nature of autonomy incorporated in autonomy-based liberalism. It is important to stress, however, that my claim is not that autonomy-based liberalism will fail because it cannot distinguish between autonomy and heteronomy: I am not suggesting that since we are all shaped by our social and moral environment, we are all more or less heteronomous and that the notion of autonomy is itself a chimaera. Rather, the force of my argument will be that autonomy-based liberalism simply cannot deliver on its promise of a plural, tolerant society in which there is a fundamental commitment to liberty: although autonomy can be distinguished from heteronomy, and although some sense can be made of the notion of full or complete autonomy (where that means what I have referred to as 'the condition of autonomy'), nevertheless such a conception will not lead to a maximally liberal, plural and tolerant society.

Autonomy and liberty

In discussing Mill's doctrine, it was suggested that the reason he fails to support as liberal a society as at first appears is because his theory of human nature generates unwelcome and illiberal consequences. The aim of this section is to suggest that modern liberalism too will be less liberal and less tolerant than it purports to be, and that this will be so despite the fact that it has officially renounced theories of human nature. If liberalism, both in its modern and in its historical forms, fails to justify a truly liberal and tolerant society, then we must look elsewhere for justifications of toleration, or must make more modest, minimalist claims for toleration. My discussion here will be divided into two parts: firstly, I shall examine liberalism's claim to justify a maximally liberal society. Secondly, I shall discuss whether liberalism justifies extensive toleration. In brief, I shall ask: 'Do liberal societies favour maximal liberty?' and 'Are liberal societies truly tolerant?'

In the previous section attention was drawn to the distinction between the condition of autonomy, which implies distance from the surrounding world, and the development and maintenance of autonomy, which requires proximity to the surrounding world. My central claim in the present section will be that even if the condition of autonomy demands the priority of liberty over other social goods, the development of autonomy will require something distinct from and in conflict with that. Moreover, since autonomy is constantly in need of development – it is always partial, never complete – it follows that liberalism may not in fact give priority to liberty over other social goods, or at least that the circumstances in which it will do so are severely limited. That the development of autonomy requires something other than maximal liberty is a point which has long been recognised, at least in general terms. In *On Liberty* Mill urges that within the restricted sphere of self-regarding action the principle of liberty applies exclusively to 'a human being arrived at the maturity of his faculties'. He concedes that 'the spirit of improvement is not always the spirit of liberty' and admits that this licenses 'temporary' and 'local' restrictions on liberty until such time as autonomy has been developed. In making this point he has in mind not only the case of children, but also 'uncivilised' nations and, sometimes, members of the working classes. In all these cases liberty may be temporarily suspended, but once the individuals arrive at the full maturity of their faculties (become autonomous) the principle of liberty will apply.

Mill's doctrine therefore depends both upon the possibility of distinguishing clearly between self-regarding and other-regarding action, and upon the possibility of distinguishing between those who are and those who are not fully autonomous. Whilst much attention has been paid to the former distinction, rather less has been said about the latter. Mill's remarks have sometimes resulted in accusations of cultural imperialism, but it is generally thought that they are mere local difficulties which can be resolved by a little judicious re-writing of his text. I doubt, however, whether the case is as simple as that: Mill's cultural imperialism seems to me to signal a profound difficulty for autonomy-based liberalism.

The difficulty is that liberalism must rely upon, yet cannot sustain, a distinction between the condition of autonomy and the development of autonomy. This distinction is needed in order to reject paternalistic interventions in the case of fully autonomous agents, but if it is to perform that function, then it must construe the autonomous agent as the possessor of a 'brave, naked will'. Conversely, if liberalism rejects the concept of autonomy as the concept of a 'brave, naked will', then it can no longer sustain the distinction between those who may and those who may not be the objects of paternalistic intervention. So liberalism must either renounce its claim to promote maximal liberty for those who are fully autonomous, or it must espouse an untenable doctrine about the nature of full autonomy.

An example of this dilemma is to be found in the writings of Mill, though again, it is not a problem which applies exclusively to Mill, but is a quite general problem for any form of autonomy-based liberalism. In Chapter IV of *On Liberty*, Mill is concerned to champion the cause of individual liberty and to argue for the widest possible area of action for people to do what they wish. To this end, he emphasises the sense in which the autonomous agent is creator of his own moral universe and urges that while 'it would be absurd to pretend that people ought to live as if nothing whatever had been known in the world before they came into it', still 'it is the privilege and proper condition of a human being, arrived at the maturity of his faculties, to use and interpret experience in his own way' (p.122).

The emphasis here is on the extent to which the autonomous agent is master of the surrounding world. The experience and learning of others are there to be employed by him and he uses them in order to discover 'what part of recorded experience is properly applicable to his own circumstances and character'. In this context Mill relies heavily on the distinction between the autonomous agent, who is active and energetic, and the non-autonomous agent who is 'inert' and 'torpid'. Throughout the discussion, the mature and autonomous man is seen as reflecting upon, critically evaluating and controlling the world in which he finds himself. That world serves the function of providing data for him, which he may use in order to establish what is best for him. Now, as has often been pointed out, this is a somewhat unrealistic picture of human nature: we are not only agents but also, and to a large extent, passive victims of the circumstances which surround us. There is no fully autonomous agent who, from a detached and impartial point of view simply surveys the world around him and draws his own conclusions from it. Yet, as we shall see, it is precisely this which Mill must imply if he is to avoid the difficulty implicit in a more realistic conception of the nature of autonomy.

In *Utilitarianism*, Mill turns to this more realistic conception. In his discussion of the distinction between higher and lower pleasures he remarks that 'capacity for the nobler feelings is in most natures a very tender plant, easily killed, not only by hostile influences but by mere want of sustenance' (Mill, 1962, p.261). Many who manage to develop these nobler feelings will do so only to lose them again, on account of the debasing effects of modern society. In this, there is a recognition that even when the condition of autonomy has been attained, it is still threatened by external factors. The autonomous agent is no longer in control of the surrounding world, using it as data for his own purposes. Rather, he is, at least in principle, a fragile creature, capable of being rendered non-autonomous by the world.

Moreover, there are illiberal implications of this aspect of Mill's account, which are often ignored, but which are highly significant. Firstly, it follows from Mill's account that the principle of liberty may apply to only a few fortunate individuals who have attained a relatively stable state of autonomy. It will not apply to the many people who have either never developed their autonomy or who have developed only a fragile and unreliable autonomy. Secondly, it follows that those restrictions on liberty which were earlier described as 'temporary' and 'local' will become far more permanent and universal if it is conceded that autonomy is something which requires continuous and sustained support. Of course, Mill does not draw these conclusions, but these are the (somewhat illiberal) conclusions which must be drawn when once the clear distinction between autonomous and non-autonomous agents is questioned.

The foregoing considerations indicate that paternalistic restrictions on liberty can be defended only if liberals assume a clear distinction between those who have total autonomy and those who do not. However, this clear distinction is neither plausible nor internally consistent with the liberal denial that there can be such a thing as a 'brave naked will', for in arguing for the distinction, liberalism assumes that fully developed autonomy is immune from the sorts of threats which attack a not-yet fully developed autonomy. In recognising the reality of those threats, however, liberalism admits that autonomy is itself something partial and incomplete.

This argument is not, I think, of the form which takes the fact of twilight to be proof that there is neither day nor night. It is not an argument designed to show that there can be no such thing as complete autonomy. Rather it is meant to suggest that the conception of autonomy which the liberal needs in order to reject paternalistic restrictions on liberty (in the case of fully autonomous agents) is in fact both implausible and inconsistent with the conception of autonomy which the liberal also needs in order to accommodate the possibility of threats to autonomy from the surrounding world. In brief, the only plausible account of full autonomy (that which recognises that it is determined in part by the surrounding world) will justify paternalistic restrictions on liberty even in the case of agents who are fully autonomous.

A further, and more general problem with the argument of autonomy-based liberalism arises out of the above considerations. This is that where autonomy is construed as something which is generated by and requires support from surrounding institutions, it may be that that fact in itself renders indeterminate the require-ment that maximal liberty be promoted. This feature of the case is one which has been discussed by Onora O'Neill who points out that 'when the institutions which define liberties and restrictions for a particular society themselves help form the capacities of members of that society for autonomous action, it is no longer possible to use a premise about the capacities for autonomous action of persons in that society in working out what the optimal set of liberties is' (O'Neill, 1979, p.56). The point here is that, even assuming that liberalism can overcome the problems inherent in justifying paternalistic action in some cases but not others, and even assuming that this justification will not involve implicit appeal to a 'brave, naked will', still where the institutions of society themselves help to form and shape autonomy, that fact may in itself make impossible the task of aiming at a maximally, or even optimally, liberal society. Of course, underpinning this objection is a firm commitment to the idea that institutions will shape and form autonomy and that the autonomous agent will not simply be in control of the world around him, but will also be influenced by that world. However, once this is admitted, then it becomes unclear whose autonomy is being discussed and it also becomes unclear what constitutes maximal or optimal liberty.

The argument of this section has been concerned to suggest that autonomy-based liberalism faces severe problems in elucidating the relationship between the autonomous individual and the surrounding world which generates his autonomy. Where that relationship is too close, serious infringements on liberty may appear to be licensed. By contrast, where the relationship is too distant, then the autonomous agent will be presented as implausibly immune to threats to autonomy. There may of course be some stable equilibrium point lying between these two extremes. Much depends here on how high we set the threshold for full autonomy. The argument is not, however, meant to show that autonomy is an irredeemably flawed concept, but only to suggest that great care is needed in appealing to it. Too often in both historical and modern liberalism, this care is not exercised and 'autonomy' is used ambiguously to imply greater or lesser distance, as required by the particular argument being employed at the time. Additionally, in an attempt to justify the liberal society as maximally liberal, liberalism may display an unrealistic neglect of the need for autonomy to be sustained, and of the institutional arrangements which are necessary preconditions of this.

In the final section of the chapter, I shall turn from the discussion of the relationship between the autonomous agent and his world, to a discussion of the relationship which holds between the autonomous agent and his own autonomy. Again, the purpose of the discussion will be to suggest that it is more difficult than it may appear for liberals to deliver on their promise of a maximally liberal and tolerant society.

Autonomy and toleration

The suggestion so far made is that autonomy-based liberalism will not necessarily foster maximal liberty and that it appears to do so only when it assumes that a clear and uncontroversial distinction can be drawn between the condition of autonomy and the development of autonomy. Some considerations have been adduced to suggest that such a distinction is far from clear and that, to the extent that that is so, the claim to promote maximal liberty is seriously undermined. However, nothing has so far been said to cast doubt on the claim that this form of liberalism will be genuinely plural and tolerant of all those many and various ways of life which do place a high value on autonomy. I turn now, therefore, to this second question, 'How plural and tolerant will autonomy-based liberalism be?'

It should first be noted that there is a problem even in phrasing the question: normally, it is proper to say that someone tolerates a particular practice or way of life only if he disapproves of that way of life. By contrast, where the way of life is one of which he approves morally, or one to which he is indifferent, then the question of toleration does not arise. Autonomy-based liberalism, however, will approve of all those forms of life which value autonomy, and therefore the question of tolerating them does not arise. What needs to be established is what the liberal attitude will be to those forms of life which do not place a high value on autonomy, and this question is most pressing in contexts in which the non-autonomous life-style takes the form of a sub-culture within the framework of a broadly liberal society. Examples of this might be the Muslim community in Britain, or the Amish community in America. The Old Order Amish share not merely a religious doctrine, but an entire way of life which is premised on the religious injunction to 'be not conformed to this world'. They seek to withdraw their children from the state education system in order to avoid their 'contamination' by outside influences, and thus they effectively deny their children the opportunity to participate in the wider society of American life. Similarly, in Britain, devout Muslims have sought to establish single sex schools for their daughters where, presumably, the ethos would not be one of independence and self-determination, but of obedience and filial loyalty. Moreover, it is not simply that, in these cases, autonomy is denied to children or to women. It is also more generally the case that independence and self-determination rank low on their list of values. Independence and self-determination are essentially the values of liberal individualism, and they are values which may well be rejected by some groups. In order, therefore, to justify its claim to be both plural and tolerant, liberalism must say something about its attitude to such groups of people – about the degree of toleration which will be extended to them and the reasons for that toleration. Here again I want to suggest that the requirement of distance, the requirement of proximity, and the recognition that autonomy can only ever be partial, combine together to undermine the liberal claim to foster a plural and tolerant society.

While it is generally recognised both that autonomous agents must stand at some distance from their own world, and that the distance can never be total, different writers give different emphasis to the requirements of distance and of proximity. This difference of emphasis corresponds to different views about the status of individual autonomy and, most importantly, about the agent's relation to his own autonomy. In what follows I shall look at two different liberal views about this relation and shall argue that neither of these provides reason for optimism that autonomy-based liberalism will generate a genuinely plural or tolerant society.

The first view is that advanced by Mill in his essay *On Liberty*. Whilst accepting that liberty may have to be suspended temporarily and locally in the case of children, barbarians or (sometimes) members of the working class, Mill nevertheless insists that those who are fully autonomous should be accorded maximal liberty. In the course of this discussion, however, he canvasses the possibility that the autonomous agent, having been provided with maximal liberty, might employ it in order to renounce the life of autonomy. The assumption here is that the agent stands at some distance even from his own autonomy, and that an autonomous life-style is itself a matter of choice, at least for agents who have attained the condition of autonomy. On Mill's view of things, then, an autonomous life is simply one amongst many. What does he have to say about the possibility that an individual might renounce the life of autonomy in favour of some other?

At this point we encounter what John Gray has referred to as 'Mill's wager'. For, in considering this possibility, Mill simply employs an optimistic view about human nature and progress to bet that it will not happen (Gray, 1983, p.70ff). Once an individual has attained autonomous status it is highly unlikely, Mill thinks, that he will voluntarily or willingly relinquish it. The point can be generalised as follows: where liberalism construes an autonomous life-style as itself the object of choice – something which might either be retained or relinquished by an autonomous agent – then there is a problem about how to respond to cases where it is relinquished. Mill simply bets optimistically that this will not in fact happen, but his optimism disguises a deep difficulty for any liberal theory which would make autonomy a matter of choice. Without the optimism, he must concede that it could, in principle, happen that an agent would prefer the non-autonomous life to the autonomous one, and at that point his structures on barbarianism become not temporary expedients, but permanent possibilities.

Thus, where autonomy is construed as merely one life-style amongst many, liberalism's refusal to be neutral as between those conceptions of life which place a high value on autonomy and those which do not, turns out to be a simple case of cultural imperialism: an unwarranted prejudice in favour of autonomous life-styles, which others may not share. The only escape from this charge of cultural imperialism is either to resort to an essentialist view of human nature, which Mill in particular, and liberals in general are reluctant to endorse, or else to engage in an inductive wager that autonomy will not in fact be discarded: that people who have tasted the delights of an autonomous life-style will be reluctant to renounce them. Mill adopts the latter strategy, but it is ultimately an unsatisfactory and, I suggest, inconsistent one. The three premises of autonomy-based liberalism which I earlier identified were:

1. The belief that the condition of autonomy requires that the agent stand at a distance from the world.
2. The belief that the development of autonomy requires that the agent be embedded in the world.
3. The belief that autonomy can only ever be partial, never complete.

If the development of autonomy can serve to justify the imposition of restrictions on liberty, and if autonomy is never fully developed, then restrictions on liberty are always possible. Such was the argument of the previous section: but if an autonomous life-style is itself a possible object of choice, then at that stage restrictions on liberty are not justifiable. Mill manages to avoid the contradiction of claiming that restriction both is and is not permissible only by assuming that, though possible, it will not be necessary since no one will willingly give up autonomy once it has been achieved. Indeed, at some points he comes close to saying that anyone who does wish to renounce autonomy cannot yet have achieved it and that, in that case, restrictions on liberty are still permissible. It seems to me that these unhappy consequences of Mill's account cannot simply be written off as problems which concern only Mill. They are in fact problems which spring directly from any account which construes an autonomous life-style as an object of choice.

Additionally, the idea that an autonomous life-style can be chosen is itself deeply puzzling. In commenting on Locke's defence of toleration I made reference to the claim that religious belief should be described in sight-analogous terms rather than volitional ones: 'seeing', 'recognising' and 'acknowledging' are the appropriate terms, not 'choosing' or 'deciding'. And so it may be with the way of life which any individual pursues. Certainly, individual decisions within our lives may be autonomously or non-autonomously made. But the idea that we may, so to speak, 'choose an autonomous life style' is paradoxical. The state of autonomy is surely the state from which I choose, not itself an object of choice.

What, then, of the alternative account, according to which the autonomous life is not itself a matter of choice, but the basis on which choices are made? Joseph Raz has recently argued, in contrast to Mill, that the condition of autonomy, once attained, cannot be renounced. An autonomous life is not, he says, one kind of life, one project or goal which may be adopted or rejected. 'For those who live in an autonomy-supporting environment there is no choice but to be autonomous' (Raz, 1986, p.391). This contrast between the location of autonomy in Mill's account and its location in Raz's account again raises the question of distance. Mill emphasises the (almost) fully autonomous agent and his distance from the social world which surrounds him: Raz, by contrast, emphasises the fact that autonomy must be developed in suitable social and institutional surroundings which cannot completely be divorced from the agent's own projects since they form the basis on which those projects are chosen. So where Mill emphasises the condition of autonomy, Raz emphasises the development of autonomy. Where Mill emphasises distance, Raz emphasises proximity. Now I am not here concerned to adjudicate between the two accounts, but simply to ask whether either can deliver on the promise of a truly tolerant and plural society. I have suggested that where distance is emphasised and autonomy is itself construed as a matter of choice, then only optimism will save the account from cultural imperialism and intolerance. Can the alternative account fare any better?

It is worth noting that Mill's solution simply is not appropriate here. Since autonomy is not a matter of choice, we cannot appeal to optimism to guarantee that it will be chosen. The location of the problem thus shifts from the autonomous agent within a liberal society to the treatment to be accorded those who live in a liberal society but who do not themselves value autonomy. Emphasising the extent to which valuable life-styles are dictated and made possible only by the institutional settings in which they are found, Raz urges not only that *we* cannot prosper in any other way than by being autonomous, but that within a liberal society *there is* no other way to prosper (Raz, 1986, p.391). This latter claim strikes at the very heart of the matter, for now there is very little reason for adopting a tolerate attitude towards members of the sub-culture, who cannot, *ex hypothesi*, enjoy a valuable non-autonomous life within a liberal society. The pluralism and tolerance which this account of liberalism affords is only between and within life styles which place a high value on autonomy. Again, we come close to Mill's society of barbarians, whose liberty must be restricted until such time as they learn to be fully autonomous, except that where it is optimism which generates Mill's conclusion that all those who come to learn autonomy will also come to value it above all else, it is pessimism about the availability of alternatives which prompts Raz's conclusion that the sub-cultures must be brought, humanely and decently, to placing value on the condition of autonomy.

Either way, it seems to me that there is here little cause for liberalism's self-professed commitment to the values of pluralism and toleration, and the difficulty is generated precisely by the inherent tension between the three notions of distance, proximity and partiality. Where distance is emphasised, then the autonomous agent may distance himself sufficiently to choose against autonomy and liberalism must contemplate its own demise or degenerate into cultural imperialism: where proximity is emphasised, then there is no valuable life within the liberal society except the life of autonomy and liberalism's claim to plurality and tolerance are undermined or radically transformed. Tolerance becomes not a virtue, but merely a temporary expedient against the day when all are autonomous.

Conclusion

In this chapter three justifications of liberalism have been considered. In each case it appears doubtful whether the justification can both account for the conceptual underpinnings of liberalism and justify its claim to promote a truly tolerant society. Scepticism has been seen to have no logically necessary or historically determinate association with toleration. Moreover, scepticism provides at best a pragmatic, not a principled defence of toleration. The neutrality argument sometimes suffers from the same defects as scepticism – indeed, sometimes collapses into scepticism – and even where it does not do so, it fails to provide an adequate analysis of liberalism's demand for neutrality, or even a clear account of what neutrality might consist in. Thus, the neutrality argument itself stands in need of justification, and that justification, I have suggested, is best found by turning to the concept of autonomy.

The concept of autonomy can, in certain circumstances, explain the precise nature of liberalism's commitment to diversity, freedom and toleration. However, the justification turns out to be something of a mixed blessing: when properly understood, it amounts to a much more restricted argument for liberty and toleration than is usually claimed. In particular, it justifies toleration only as an instrumental value, and only within very restricted limits. In some respects, the arguments I have presented against autonomy-based liberalism echo the arguments which were first presented against Locke's account of toleration in his seventeenth-century *Letter*. Autonomy-based liberalism ultimately contains no commitment to the value of diversity in and of itself. It justifies only those diverse forms of life which themselves value autonomy and thus makes toleration a pragmatic device – a temporary expedient – not a matter of principle.

In the next chapter I shall re-examine the commitment to

neutrality incorporated in many liberal theories. The strategy here will be to consider what is involved in construing neutrality as the guiding model, rather than the theoretical foundation of liberalism, and my conclusion will be that here too modern liberalism is far less tolerant in practice than its advocates would have us believe.

5 Toleration in a Liberal Society

'The best lack all conviction'

The conclusion of the previous chapter – that autonomy-based liberalism is far less open, plural and tolerant than its advocates would have us believe – is a somewhat surprising and contentious one. Characteristically, liberals are accused of displaying too much tolerance, not too little. They are said to be far too ready to welcome diverse ways of life, and far too reluctant to suppress unacceptable forms of behaviour. Hence the accusation that liberals aspire to indifference: 'The best lack all conviction, whilst the worst are full of passionate intensity.' Hence too the fact that liberals are required constantly to 'distinguish between permission and praise, between allowing a practice and endorsing it' (Sandel, 1984, p.1). For example, they must adhere strictly to the distinction between permitting pornographic material and approving of it. Similarly, they must be clear about the difference between defending free speech and defending the opinions expressed in the exercise of free speech. Like Voltaire, they need not agree with what others say, even though they defend to the death their right to say it. Of necessity, toleration involves dislike or disapproval of the thing tolerated, and the liberal must be mindful of the distinction between, on the one hand, toleration and unbridled licence and, on the other, toleration and apathy, if permission is not to be interpreted as praise, nor indifference to be confused with toleration.

These considerations raise the question which will be considered in this chapter 'What will the liberal society be committed to in practice?' For even if liberals do adhere strictly to the distinction between permission and praise, or tolerance and licence, it may still be argued that they are willing to tolerate that which is intolerable: that they extend toleration to practices and beliefs which should be outlawed. Sometimes it is held that this is because liberals are genuinely 'over tolerant' – they tolerate the intolerable. At other times it is held that this is because liberal societies have no beliefs or values at all: they appear to be tolerant, but in fact the apparent toleration is a manifestation of official indifference. 'Here come the liberals, with their stirring battle cry, "On the one hand . . . on the other hand . . .".' We need to ask, therefore, 'What kind of society do liberals favour?' 'What vision of the ideal state are they embracing?'

Before embarking on this discussion, it is important to bear in mind exactly what the previous chapter claims to have shown. In examining different justifications of toleration, it was argued that the autonomy-based defence has special status: it is a defence which is uniquely liberal and not available to writers in other traditions. It captures 'the spirit of the liberal approach to politics'. What was meant by this was that liberalism is characterised by its commitment to individual self-determination. What matters is not (or not simply) that people should be possessed of the truth, but that they should find their own way to the truth – that they should be part creators of their own lives. To quote Mill again, a person's 'own mode of laying out his existence is best, not because it is best in itself, but because it is his own mode' (Mill, 1978, p.133). Toleration is then required in order that people should have and develop individual autonomy.

The limitation of this, however, was the case of those societies or sub-groups within society which do not so value autonomy, and the charge against liberalism was not that it denied toleration to such groups, but that it interpreted toleration as a necessary evil in their case, not a genuine good. This, I suggested, is a conclusion which ought to worry liberals, primarily because it appears to take us back to the more pragmatic defences of toleration which were earlier found to be inadequate and which modern liberalism claimed to transcend. The kinds of criticism levelled at scepticism and discussed in Chapter 4 emphasise that it is not sufficient simply to tolerate. Toleration must also be correctly grounded. In particular, it must be grounded in respect for persons and their autonomy, not in considerations of expediency. It turned out, however, that this could be done only for those ways of life which

themselves value autonomy. For the rest, liberals are forced
into precisely the pragmatic defences of toleration which were
previously held to be inadequate. Thus, the charge against autonomy-based liberalism is not the simple charge that it fails to be
sufficiently tolerant, but rather that it fails to accord the proper
status to toleration in the case of those individuals or groups which
do not value autonomy. It fails to deliver on its promise of a
society which will construe and extend toleration as a genuine
good.

All this, however, is at the purely conceptual level, and liberals
might well respond by claiming that in practice there will be only
a very small number of cases in which autonomy is not valued and
that, in those cases, liberals need not feel too embarrassed, since
toleration must have limits as well as grounds. No one, however
liberal, need extend unlimited toleration to all forms of life and
modes of behaviour. Much less are liberals committed to seeing
value in every form of life, however it is based. More generally,
liberals might deny that what unites them is any sort of conceptual
foundation at all. Like Ackerman, they are willing to identify
many highways to the liberal state, many 'plausible paths to
Neutrality' (Ackerman, 1980, p.11).

This response suggests a different approach to liberalism, which
will form the basis of discussion in this chapter. The earlier
discussion sought to characterise all forms of liberalism as sharing
a common conceptual foundation. It implied that that common
foundation was what united liberals. However, Ackerman's
approach suggests that the common link might lie in what liberals
are for rather than why they are for it. What unites liberals, on
this view, is not some commitment to a single foundational value –
such as autonomy, or liberty, or equality – but rather a shared
picture of how states should conduct themselves. There is no single
basic value of liberalism, but only a general picture of how liberal
states will behave. The common feature is not what liberals believe
at the philosophical level, but what they aspire to at the practical
level. 'A liberal state is envisaged as one in which people will
practice and pursue a variety of opposing and incommensurable
life styles' (Waldron, 1987, p.144). 'Liberals resolve not to favour
any particular ends, or to impose on citizens a preferred way of
life' (Sandel, 1984, p.3). Liberalism endorses 'an image of society
as a neutral arena' (Miller, 1988, p.239).

These quotations re-introduce a concept which has been referred to (somewhat dismissively) earlier in this book – the concept of neutrality. However, whereas the Chapter 4 discussion focused upon neutrality as the conceptual foundation of liberalism, this chapter will concentrate upon it as a practical aim of the liberal society – as answering questions about what liberals are for, rather than why they are for it.

The distinction between neutrality as a philosophical foundation of liberalism and neutrality as a guiding political aim of liberalism will involve discussion of practical cases in which questions of toleration arise. Such discussion is pertinent because justifications of legal and social reform have frequently been made in terms of neutrality. Thus, for example, arguments about the permissibility of pornography, about the propriety of race relations legislation, and about educational reform in multi-cultural societies, have all been couched in terms of a requirement to be neutral between competing conceptions of the good. I shall discuss different interpretations of the neutrality requirement, and examine the different practical policies which they dictate. Finally, I shall examine the implications of this, and the Chapter 4 argument, for liberalism generally. My tentative conclusion will again be that it cannot deliver on its promise of a truly tolerant society: the argument of Chapter 4 shows that in theory liberals do not accord the right status to groups which do not themselves value autonomy. The argument of this chapter aims to show that in practice the limits of toleration are ambiguously and indeterminately drawn within liberal society.

The principle of neutrality

The concept of neutrality has appeared several times, and in several different guises, in the course of this book. In Chapter 4 neutrality was referred to as a possible conceptual foundation of liberalism, and it was argued there that it failed, in itself, to provide an adequate foundation because, in the absence of further detail, neutrality is too vague and ambiguous a term to do the philosophical work required of it: for example, the demand for neutrality is ambiguous between neutrality in outcome (as favoured by Dworkin) and neutrality in motivation (as favoured by Locke and Mill). Similarly, it was unclear whether being neutral meant standing back and doing nothing, or whether it implied intervention and active attempts to equalise opportunity. To choose between these conflicting interpretations, it was argued, we need some understanding of why neutrality is thought to be desirable in the first place, and that understanding can be obtained only by looking at a deeper principle than the neutrality principle, such as the principle of autonomy. The nature of the neutrality advocated is then determined by this deeper principle, and not something which can be understood independently of it. The concept of neutrality is under-determined, ambiguous – even vacuous – unless explained by reference to a more fundamental principle.

It may appear from this that neutrality is a concept which liberals would do best to forget, but to think that would be a mistake. The argument of Chapter 4 has shown only that neutrality alone cannot provide a conceptual foundation for liberalism, not that neutrality as a practical aim or guiding vision is disreputable. Moreover, the appeal of a principle of neutrality is powerful and all-pervasive. As Bruce Ackerman puts it; 'It is not enough to reject one or another of the basic arguments that lead to a reasoned commitment to neutrality; one must reject *all* of them. And to do this does not require a superficial change of political opinions but a transform-ation of one's entire view of the world' (Ackerman, 1980, p.12). Neutrality as a political perspective survives attempts to undermine its conceptual foundation. This may be because there is no single, conceptual foundation. It may be because the search for a foundation was misconceived from the start: we should not attempt to discover what justifies appeal to neutrality, but rather what dangers neutrality guards against. Instead of dismissing neutrality as an ambiguous and inadequately supported philosophical foun-dation, we should instead construe it as a guiding political principle. But what exactly is meant by this appeal to the distinction between neutrality as the conceptual foundation and neutrality as the practical political aim of liberalism?

Neutrality: concept and practice

Three major contributors to modern liberal political theory are John Rawls, Bruce Ackerman and Ronald Dworkin. What is remarkable about these three is that whilst each provides a different conceptual underpinning for liberalism, each also subscribes to an ideal of the liberal state as neutral between competing conceptions of the good life. That is to say, they give different answers to the question 'What is the justification of liberalism?' but they give broadly similar answers to the question 'What is the liberal state aiming at in its practical policies?' A few brief quotations from their writings will go some way to explaining this distinction.

In his article, 'Liberalism', Ronald Dworkin asserts that:

> 'Political decisions must be, so far as is possible, independent of any particular conception of the good life, or of what gives value to life. Since the citizens of a society differ in their conceptions [of what the good life consists in], the government does not treat them as equals if it prefers one conception to another, either because the officials believe that one is intrinsically superior, or because one is held by the more numerous or powerful group.' (Dworkin, 1985, p.191)

Dworkin's requirement of neutrality in practical politics is determined by his belief that liberalism is founded on a view of persons as entitled to equal concern and respect. And what that dictates is that the practical policies of the liberal state should be such as to be neutral between diverse and competing conceptions of the good. Equality is the philosophical foundation of liberalism, but neutrality is its normal practical consequence. It is what liberal policies aspire to attain.

Turning from Dworkin to Ackerman, we find a similar commitment to neutrality in practical politics, but this time the requirement has a different rationale. As has been noted already, Ackerman countenances a variety of different possible ways of grounding liberal commitment to neutrality. He says:

> 'In proposing neutrality I do not imagine I am defending an embattled citadel on the fringe of modern civilisation. Instead, I am pointing to a place well within the cultural interior that can be reached by countless pathways of argument coming from very different directions. As time passes, some paths are abandoned while others are worn smooth; yet the exciting work

on the frontier cannot blind us to the hold that the center has upon us.' (Ackerman, 1980, p.12)

According to Ackerman, then, neutrality is crucial to liberal political practice, but he appears indifferent as to how we arrive at a justification for it. Policies must be neutral, but there is no single argument forcing the move to neutrality, only a variety of different arguments, having more or less appeal at different times and to different people. Ackerman shares with Dworkin a commitment to the need for governments to display neutrality in their practical policies, though he does not share with Dworkin a whole-hearted commitment to the principle of equal concern and respect as *the* justifying principle of neutrality. (I say that Ackerman 'appears' indifferent, because it is unclear whether he is as hostile to egalitarianism as he would have us believe. His precise formulation of the neutrality principle prohibits any person from asserting that he or his conception of the good is better than anyone else or their conception of the good. In practice, this seems to amount to a theory not dissimilar to Dworkin's – not dissimilar to the claim that all people must be treated with equal concern and respect.)

In John Rawls' *Theory of Justice* the situation is slightly different again: Rawls writes a requirement of neutrality into the original position from which decisions are to be taken. On his account, governments will be neutral as between competing conceptions of the good because, from the original position, no one will be possessed of the relevant information necessary to generate non-neutrality. No one will know his own conception of the good and therefore no one will be in a position to impose that conception of the good on others. Rawls' account depends, in part, upon a Kantian conception of persons as autonomous agents, and thus his commitment to neutrality may be seen as springing from a view of persons as commanding and deserving of 'mutual respect and self esteem'. 'The original position,' he says, 'may be viewed as a procedural interpretation of Kant's conception of autonomy and the categorical imperative' (Rawls, 1971, p.256).

(Again, although Rawls' explanation differs from Dworkin's, it is also similar to it in important ways. Officially, Dworkin rejects autonomy as a possible conceptual foundation for liberalism, arguing that autonomy is merely 'another name for neutrality', and that since neutrality cannot ground liberalism, neither can autonomy. Nevertheless, his own justification, in terms of equal concern and respect, has a not dissimilar Kantian ancestry.)

These brief references to the theories of Dworkin, Ackerman and Rawls are obviously very crude and partial. Nevertheless, they serve to indicate that some of the most powerful voices in modern liberalism are united in their commitment to the need for neutrality, even if divided in their accounts of what justifies it or of what it consists in. Neutrality is held to be the practical manifestation of liberalism, even if not its conceptual foundation. But what does neutrality require of us? What is it exactly for a state to be neutral and, most importantly for our purposes, where are the proper limits of state neutrality?

In what follows I shall discuss alternative interpretations of the neutrality principle, construed as a practical aim of politics. In particular, I shall isolate two problem areas for that principle and draw some connections between those problem areas and practical problems of toleration. The areas may be identified by the two questions: 'What is the *scope* of the neutrality principle?' and 'What are the *requirements* of neutrality?' Questions about scope are questions about the sorts of things neutralists are neutral between; questions about the requirements of neutrality are questions about the sorts of policies governments are committed to implementing if they are to claim to be neutral.

The scope of the neutrality principle

I noted earlier Brian Barry's claim that 'liberalism incorporates the idea that the state is an instrument for satisfying the wants men happen to have, rather than a means of making good men.' In similar vein Jeremy Waldron states that 'a liberal society is envisaged as one in which people will practice and pursue a variety of opposing and incommensurable life-styles', and Robert Nozick also urges that 'A state or government that claims . . . allegiance scrupulously must be neutral between its citizens.' This picture of a liberal society (some would count it the defining feature of a liberal society) is of a neutral arena within which a great variety of different and opposing ways of life may be pursued. It is not the role of the state to adjudicate between these opposing ways of life, but only to provide a framework within which they may be pursued freely. Thus, within a liberal state, Christians, Jews, agnostics, atheists, Muslims, Buddhists may all equally well pursue the way of life dictated by their religion (or lack of it). Similarly, the liberal state will be neutral between lovers of classical music, lovers of rock music, lovers of jazz, and the tone deaf.

Again, it is important to note that these claims are not, and do not purport to be, explanations of the foundations of liberalism: rather, they are pictures, or models, of how the liberal society conducts itself – of what it aims at in its application, not what it is based on in its theory; of what it believes to be a proper political order, not why it takes that order to be proper. As one writer has recently put it;

> 'Neutralists conceive the state as having an essentially secondary role in the lives of its citizens. A referee in a game of football does not himself play football. He simply administers the rules within which others play the game. Similarly, the state is not itself to pursue the good life – whatever that may be – ; it is simply to establish and maintain the ground rules within which others can engage in that pursuit'. (Jones, 1989)

This mention of ground rules introduces an important limiting condition of government neutrality. Like the football referee, the liberal state is not committed to a policy of complete and unrestricted laissez faire. Both the state and the referee allow freedom only within certain prescribed limits. In the case of the referee, there is freedom within the rules of the game; in the case of the state, there is freedom within the laws.

This may seem an obvious, even trivial point. Under any plausible interpretation, the requirement that the state shall be neutral is not a requirement that it shall be neutral between absolutely everything which people might want, or between everything which they might perceive as contributing to their conception of the good. It is only a requirement that *within limits* it shall be neutral. Although committed to being neutral between opera lovers and rock concert lovers, the neutral state is not committed to displaying neutrality with respect to arsonists or rapists. The laws which we have against arson and against rape do, of course, militate against anyone whose conception of the good includes the desirability of burning property or raping women, but it would be absurd to claim that a state fails in neutrality simply because it is not even-handed in its treatment of such people. (This, of course, is not to deny that the state must provide fair trials for people accused of rape or arson. It is only to point out that neutrality does not require construing a life devoted to arson as just as legitimate as a life devoted to jazz or a life devoted to Buddhism.) However, this apparently obvious point is the source of a considerable conceptual problem for liberalism, and one which has consequences for its attempts to define the scope of neutrality and to identify the demands of toleration in a liberal society.

In modern political philosophy a distinction is often made between the right and the good, and arguments are adduced for the priority of the right over the good. That is to say, it is often claimed that there is a conception of the right which specifies the limits within which people may be allowed to pursue their own conception of the good. Such a distinction is integral to neutralist liberalism, for in so far as it advocates official government neutrality between competing conceptions of the good, it implicitly assumes that we can first delineate the area of the right, and then move on to resolving questions about the good life and the forms it may take. On this view, the concept of right demarcates the area within which government interference may (though it need not) be legitimate; the concept of the good demarcates the area in which people should be free from government interference. 'The principles of right, and so of justice, put limits on which satisfactions have value; they impose restrictions on what are the reasonable conceptions of one's good . . . we can express this by saying that the concept of right is prior to that of good' (Rawls, 1971, p.31). A similar distinction is appealed to by Ronald Dworkin when he insists that rights are 'trumps' in politics. Questions about the good may be variously answered, but they are all silenced when considerations of right are in the air, and considerations of right are prior to and independent of considerations of good. However, these claims – that the right may be so clearly distinguished from the good, and that the right has priority over the good, are highly debatable. In particular, it is sometimes argued that the place at which we choose to draw a line between the right and the good will itself be determined by our conception of the good. The concept of right, far from being (as the liberal insists) independent of and anterior to any conception of the good, will in fact be a function of our conception of the good.

If correct, this criticism has far-reaching implications for the possibility of identifying the scope of the neutrality principle. That principle urges neutrality *between competing conceptions of the good*, but the burden of the criticism is to suggest that there is no such thing as a conception of the good independent of the interpretation of neutrality itself.

In order to explain and assess the criticism I shall return briefly to Mill and to his requirement that 'the sole reason for which power can be rightfully exercised over any member of a community . . . is to prevent harm to others.' The reasons for returning to Mill are two-fold: firstly to fulfil an earlier promise to discuss his account of restrictions on liberty (to discuss the negative as well as the positive claims he makes). Secondly, to examine the harm principle as a principle of political neutrality. Mill's distinction between harm and offence is often seen as an important precursor of modern distinctions between the right and good. Both Mill and modern liberals seek to specify the scope of the neutrality principle – the justifiable limits of state neutrality. Mill does this by reference to the concept of harm and its place within a utilitarian moral theory. Many modern liberals, impressed by the defects of utilitarianism, attempt to define the limits by reference to more Kantian notions. In particular, the distinction between the right and the good. However, both Mill and modern liberals believe that there is a clear and uncontroversial way of differentiating between areas in which legislation is (in principle) permissible, and areas where it is not. This belief is, however, highly contentious;

> 'the liberal's argument is that the basis of legislation should be the prevention of harm to others, and that within this limitation the law should not seek to enforce or protect any particular moral point of view. However, the cogency of the liberal's position will depend upon the plausibility of an uncontroversial conception of harm, for, if what is thought to be harmful is internally connected to particular moral perspectives, then the liberal's position can be seen to be deeply flawed.' (Horton, 1985, pp.116–17)

The scope of neutrality and Mill's harm principle

In stating the 'simple principle' of *On Liberty* Mill urges that an individual;

> 'cannot rightfully be compelled to do or forbear because it will be better for him to do so, because it will make him happier, because in the opinions of others, to do so would be wise or even right. These are good reasons for remonstrating with him, or reasoning with him, or persuading him, or entreating him, but not for compelling him or visiting him with any evil in case he do otherwise.' (Mill, 1978, p.68)

Harm – specifically harm to others – is the sole warrant for government interference in Mill's opinion. The limits of individual liberty are set by reference to the concept of harm, and the legitimate areas of government intervention are similarly circumscribed by it. Governments must tolerate those actions which cause offence, distress, or outrage, and may interfere only in cases where the actions threaten harm to others – and not always then. It is by appeal to the concept of harm that Mill hopes to set the limits of state neutrality. But what criterion is to be applied in determining whether an action has in fact caused harm to another? Notoriously, Mill's principle is open to a multitude of interpretations, many of them inconsistent with one another, and some of them illiberal in their implications. In his book *Mill on Liberty: A Defence* John Gray raises some of the many questions which bedevil Mill's concept of harm;

> 'Does he [Mill] intend the reader to understand "harm" to refer only to physical harm, or must a class of moral harms to character be included in any application of the liberty principle? Must the harm that the restriction of liberty prevents be done directly to identifiable individuals, or may it also relevantly be done to institutions, social practices and forms of life? Can serious offence to feelings count as harm so far as the restriction of liberty is concerned . . .? Can a failure to benefit someone, or to perform one's obligations to the public, be construed as a case in which harm is done?' (Gray, 1983, p.49)

Depending on how we answer these questions, the scope of the term 'harm' may be more or less wide, more or less value-laden, and more or less controversial. In this section I shall discuss those aspects of Mill's principle which I earlier referred to as the 'negative' elements. My aim will be to indicate that for Mill, and also for modern liberals, the scope of neutrality is profoundly ambiguous and certainly not value-free. This, moreover, is not an exercise in textual analysis, but rather a general claim to the effect that the principle of neutrality is not value-free, but value-laden.

However, before embarking on that project, it is important to establish that Mill's harm principle is indeed an example of the principle of neutrality. Referring to Mill, Joseph Raz remarks;

'The doctrine of political neutrality claims that (some) political actions should be neutral regarding ideals of the good life, that implementation or promotion of ideals of the good life is, though worthy in itself, not a legitimate ground for (some) political actions. Such a doctrine is a doctrine of restraint since (as understood here) it advocates neutrality between valid and invalid ideals of the good alike. It demands not only that the promotion of unacceptable ideals should not be the ground for (some) political actions, but also that the promotion of acceptable, correct, desirable ideals should be equally shunned.' (Raz, 1982, p.91)

That Mill subscribes to a principle of neutrality (so understood) is clear from his statement of the simple principle, in which he warns against compelling an individual to some action because 'to do so would be wise or even right'. Thus, in the political sphere admirable ideals are to be shunned just as much as repugnant ones. His principle is a principle of restraint which operates indifferently with respect to good and bad ideals. Moreover, underpinning Mill's commitment to a principle of neutrality is the belief that a distinction can be drawn between the imposition of an ideal and the prevention of harm. The latter is (at least sometimes) good reason for intervention; the former can never be. How then does Mill propose to distinguish between actions which cause harm and actions which do not? More generally, can any clear distinction be drawn at all between actions which cause harm and actions which merely provoke offence, disgust, or disapproval? Or (alternatively) are actions which provoke offence, disgust or disapproval themselves harmful?

One very familiar area in which these questions arise in modern politics, and an area in which Mill's principle has been explicitly appealed to, is that of legislation governing the availability of obscene or pornographic literature. The 1979 *Report of the Committee on Obscenity and Film Censorship* (The Williams Committee) appeals directly to Mill in advocating that 'no conduct should be suppressed by law unless it can be shown to harm someone', and the Committee further elaborates this principle by insisting that 'harm' here means 'actual physical harm'. But if we generalise this interpretation it appears to deliver a principle which is far too strong: all kinds of actions are outlawed in British and American society despite the fact that they do not cause actual physical harm. For example, and as Ronald Dworkin has pointed out, there are regulations forbidding the commercial development of certain parts of cities, or restricting the private use of natural resources, like the sea-shore. Similarly, laws of libel and of slander cannot pass the harm test if it is construed in this way, and neither can laws governing conspiracy or blasphemy (Dworkin, 1985, p.336).

On the other hand, if 'harm' is more weakly construed, so as to include moral harm, or offence, or mental distress, or upset, then it becomes too weak, since (to quote Dworkin again) 'any kind of conduct likely to be made criminal in a democracy is conduct that causes annoyance and distress to someone' (ibid.). So either 'harm' is construed so narrowly that it fails to justify restriction on actions which we would certainly wish to restrict, or it is construed so widely that it may be used to justify endless interference and almost unlimited legislative powers.

These objections to the harm principle are familiar and powerful. However, what I wish to draw attention to here is an implication of them which is often inadequately recognised. Faced with a choice between the narrow and the wide interpretations of harm, commentators often assume (and the Williams Report also assumes) that it is clear what constitutes a harm, but less clear whether the law should restrict itself to harms, or whether it should also feel free to range across offence, mental distress, moral disapproval and the like. However, an alternative interpretation seems to me more plausible. In cases in which there is controversy over the

proper extent of legislative interference, it is quite as likely to be
the case that people differ over what consitutes a harm: they differ
over the scope of the term 'harm', and thus over the scope of the
neutrality principle. So it is not necessarily the case that we all
understand what harms are, but are unsure whether the law should
restrict itself to them alone. Rather, we are divided from the outset
about what harm essentially is. And this disagreement, far from
being merely linguistic, has its origin in deeply held moral beliefs.
Reflecting on the recommendations of the Williams Committee,
Dworkin remarks;

> 'Suppose "harm" is taken to exclude mental distress, but to
> include damage to the social and cultural environment. Then
> the harm condition is in itself no help in considering the problem
> of pornography, because opponents of pornography argue, with
> some force, that free traffic in obscenity does damage the general
> cultural environment.' (Dworkin, 1985, p.337)

Dworkin's point is well made. His reference to unhelpfulness
betrays his belief that there is an alternative way of delimiting the
scope of the neutrality principle. He believes that appeal to harm
is 'no help' because the concept of harm will not provide a
satisfactory criterion for state intervention. He nevertheless thinks
that such a criterion can be provided, namely his own criterion in
terms of rights. Talk of harm will not serve to define the scope of
the neutrality principle, but some other, rights-based account will.
The rights-based approach will be considered in the next section.
Here, I shall discuss the precise problem with the harm principle.

The unhelpfulness of the harm principle can be seen by considering Andrea Dworkin's famous claim 'pornography *is* violence
against women' (A. Dworkin, 1981). Unlike the members of the
Williams Committee, she construes 'harm' as ranging wider than
the purely physical. She is not arguing that the incidence of rape,
mugging and physical violence against women increases statistically
with the proliferation of pornography and that, in that sense,
pornography *causes* physical harm. Rather, her claim is precisely
that it is harmful in itself and independent of its specific consequences. Dworkin's belief, and her complaint, is that even where
empirical evidence is lacking pornography is nevertheless a form
of violence against women, since it exploits and subjugates them.

She believes it to be corrupt and she wants it not to exist (Mendus, 1985, pp.99–112).

At this point it might be salutory to recall Mary Warnock's claim 'The intolerable is the unbearable. And we may simply feel, believe, conclude without reason that something is unbearable and must be stopped' (Warnock, 1987, p.126). That claim was made in the context of a denial that there can be any general distinction between moral judgements, which are based on reason, and non-moral judgements, which are based on feeling. But a similar point can be made in this context too: just as there may be no clear line between the moral and the non-moral, so there may be no clear line between what is harmful and what is not. My assessment of what is harmful may be essentially informed by my moral beliefs, not prior to and independent of them. If, like Andrea Dworkin, I believe pornographic material to be corrupt in itself, I will think it a great harm that it exists. If not, not. And the liberal aspiration to delineate an uncontroversial and value-free concept of harm is thus highly contentious.

However, hard cases make bad law, and it might be said that the above arguments indicate only, and at most, that there are 'grey areas' in which the concept of harm is value-laden. They do not show that there is no 'core' sense of 'harm' which is value-neutral. It may therefore be thought that even if 'harm' is a concept which is fuzzy at the edges, it will still serve to identify central cases in which legislation may be permissible. But even this, minimalist, account has been questioned.

At one level, it may seem clear what constitutes a harm: physical injury, death, and imprisonment are frequently cited as paradigm cases of harms, but even these are not always and invariably perceived as harms by the people who experience them. On the contrary, death may be seen as a blessed release; imprisonment as a cleansing experience; and physical injury as necessary for spiritual and moral improvement. A classic case of the last is the attitude of (at least some) Muslim women to so-called female circumcision. From a western perspective, we see this practice as barbaric mutilation, but there is every reason to believe that the women themselves construe the matter differently, regarding it rather as harmful not to undergo such treatment. We may dissent from this opinion and abhor the view of female sexuality which it implies, but that is not the question here. The question is whether female circumcision necessarily constitutes a harm, and the answer is that it does not, or at least that whether it does depends crucially upon the moral perspective from which it is viewed. In this context, to describe it as mutilation is question-begging. As one writer has put it; 'it is misleading to say that mutilation is a paradigm case of harm for though there may be general agreement that "mutilation" is harmful, this may obscure serious and deep disagreements about what is to count as mutilation' (Horton, 1985, p.121). More generally, the point is this: we may agree with Mill that all and only those actions which are harmful are candidates for legal restriction or prohibition, but such agreement hardly constitutes a useful criterion, for it disguises deep moral disagreement about what exactly is to count as a harm – and this is so even in ostensibly 'paradigm' cases.

The right and the good

I mentioned earlier Ronald Dworkin's rejection of the harm principle on the grounds that it is 'not helpful'. He claims, with some plausibility, that disagreements about the status of pornography are not likely to be resolved via the principle. Dworkin can afford to be sanguine about this conclusion, for he believes that he has an alternative, and superior, method of specifying the scope of the neutrality principle. This is a rights-based argument, which he himself presents not merely as an alternative argument, but an alternative *strategy* for settling questions about the limits of state intervention. His complaint against the harm principle is not merely that it is ambiguous and indeterminate, but also (and more importantly) that it provides 'contingent reasons for convictions that we do not hold contingently' (Dworkin, 1985, p.352). In brief, he construes the harm principle as a goal-based strategy – a strategy which looks to the long-term beneficial consequences of permitting free speech and free availability of pornography. But such a strategy is, he says 'just silly'.

'Very few of those who defend peoples' right to read pornography in private would actually claim that the community or the individual is better off with more pornography rather than less. So a goal-based argument for pornography must do without what seem the strongest (though still contingent) strands in the goal-based argument for free speech.' (Ibid)

It is thus the utilitarian overtones of the harm principle which Dworkin is most concerned about. As an alternative to this strategy, he presents a rights-based defence of pornography. He says;

'the right to moral independence requires a permissive legal attitude toward the consumption of pornography in private . . . the right of moral independence is part of the same collection of rights as the right of political independence, and it is to be justified as a trump over an unrestricted utilitarian defence of prohibitory laws against pornography, in a community of those who find offence just in the idea that their neighbours are reading dirty books.' (p.358)

At root, it is the right to be treated with equal concern and respect which Dworkin values most, and which he believes will dictate a liberal attitude towards the circulation of pornographic material. Everything depends, therefore, on his ability to show *both* that the harm principle fails to respect the right of moral independence, *and* that his own rights-based strategy is superior in this respect. But what reason is there for thinking that the rights-based strategy will not encounter precisely the indeterminacies which plagued the harm principle?

The objection to the harm principle was not simply that it provided contingent reasons for convictions that we do not hold contingently. It was rather that it failed to provide reasons for action at all: the burden of my criticism of the harm principle was that there is no value-free account of what constitutes a harm. Is there then an acceptable account of what the right to moral independence consists in, or of what constitutes treatment as an equal? Dworkin apparently thinks so. Whilst accepting that some objections to the availability of pornography might be morally grounded, he nevertheless concludes that the right to moral independence requires a permissive legal attitude toward the consumption of pornography in private. This right may be overridden only if *serious* damage can be shown to follow from it. If, for example, it can be shown that the private consumption of

pornography significantly increases the incidence of violent crime
or of sexual offences (p.354). It cannot be over-ridden simply
because people believe (perhaps correctly) that reading pornographic material is demeaning or bestial or morally corrupt.

The problems with this strategy are two-fold: firstly, by appealing
to 'serious damage' as the only appropriate ground for suspending
the right, Dworkin reverts to the concept of harm which he earlier
found so unhelpful. He takes 'damage' to refer to physical damage –
the increase in violent crime, or increase in sex offences consequent
upon the availability of pornography. But as we have seen, those
who object to pornography need not hold a causal view of this
sort. And if Dworkin rules their objections out of court (as he
does), then the second problem arises – namely, whether their
right of moral independence is not violated by the availability of
pornography.

In December 1983 the Minneapolis City Council approved a
new ordinance which declares that 'certain kinds of pornography
violate women's rights'. The rationale of the ordinance (drafted
by Andrea Dworkin and Catherine MacKinnon) was to draw
attention to the belief that pornography is a matter of civil rights,
not a matter of causal connections and empirical evidence. Susanne
Kappeler puts the point this way:

> 'The censorship experts are asking for proof that men who have
> looked at pornography will go and do something similar (to the
> "content") in the world . . . What the men are doing in the
> world is continuing to *see* – to see women as objects of their
> pleasure and their feeling of life. It is quite enough "behaviour"
> in my opinion.' (Kappeler, 1986, p.60)

Thus, viewed from the perspective of the would-be consumer of
pornography, the principle of moral independence dictates a policy
of toleration. Viewed from the feminist perspective it dictates a
policy of restriction. Ronald Dworkin is at least partly conscious of
these difficulties. He concedes that 'we are trying to discover, not
an algorithm for a law of obscenity, but rather whether a plausible
abstract right will yield a sensible scheme of regulation' (p.357).
Yet even this is doubtful: there is not one plausible abstract right
suggested by the problem of pornography, but two. There are the
rights of the would-be consumer, and the rights of (at least some)

women. These rights simply conflict, and not only is there no algorithm for a sensible law governing pornography, there is no more than appeal to the concept of harm which has already been seen to be deeply flawed. At root, the rights-based strategy is no more helpful than the goal-based strategy, since in each case appeal must ultimately be made to a concept of 'harm' or of 'serious damage' which is itself value-laden.

The test of neutrality

The upshot of the foregoing argument is to suggest that the liberal attempt to attain neutrality is seriously undermined by difficulties inherent in specifying the scope of the term 'harm'. This difficulty, moreover, is one which besets a rights-based strategy just as much as a goal-based strategy. Thus, the liberal claim to neutrality, founded upon the possibility of differentiating between the right and the good, suffers from indeterminacy of scope, and in consequence of this, attempts to specify the limits of toleration will similarly be beset by difficulties. What, then, of the other problem mentioned at the beginning of the chapter – the problem of identifying the requirements of neutrality, or of deciding when a political policy is in fact neutral?

In order to explain this problem more clearly I shall appeal to two further distinctions within neutrality – intentional and causal conceptions of neutrality; and positive and negative senses of neutrality. The former (which was briefly referred to in Chapter 4) is concerned with the distinction between neutrality in reasons and neutrality in outcomes; the latter is concerned with the precise nature of neutrality in outcomes and what that amounts to.

Intentional and causal neutrality

The distinction between intentional and causal neutrality operates on the assumption (which may, of course, be unfounded) that we have already identified the class of actions to which a principle of neutrality applies – i.e. that we have some rough distinction between the right and the good. Working on that assumption, we may then ask; 'Within the area of the good, does neutrality apply to reasons for action or does it apply to consequences of action? Should we insist that policies be neutral simply in the reasons which they adopt for prevention or suppression, or is something more extensive required?' This reference to neutrality with respect to reasons takes us back to Locke and his claim that religious practices should not be outlawed simply on the grounds that they are religiously motivated. He says:

> 'But if peradventure such were the state of things, that the Interest of the Commonwealth required all slaughter of Beasts should be forborn for some while, in order to the increasing of the stock of Cattel, that had been destroyed by some extraordinary Murrain; Who sees not that the Magistrate, in such a case, may forbid all his Subjects to kill any Calves for any use whatsoever? Only 'tis to be observed, that in this case the Law is not made about a Religious, but a Political matter: nor is the Sacrifice, but the Slaughter of Calves thereby prohibited.' (Locke, 1983, p.42)

On Locke's account, we have no right to freedom of worship as such but only, and at most, a right not to have our worship interfered with for religious ends. Generalising, we may say that this is a requirement of neutrality in intention – a requirement that governments not aim at disbenefiting certain groups of people simply because they have a particular conception of the good. (Again, this requirement clearly implies that we can discriminate between the right and the good.)

In discussing this question earlier, I alluded to the common complaint that such a conception of neutrality invites sophistry of one form or another: it is notoriously difficult to establish what the motivation is behind any particular piece of legislation and, given this fact, neutrality in motivation may simply be the fig leaf with which to disguise antagonism towards a particular group or groups. Ways of life may wither away and die not because they are clearly and overtly legislated against, but as a result of the unintended, though forseeable, consequences of some kinds of legislation.

On the other hand, however, requiring neutrality in outcome may be asking the impossible. The example cited earlier was that of Sunday trading laws, and it was suggested there that to have some restriction on trading would be to favour the Christian over the atheist, whereas to have no restriction would be to favour the atheist over the Christian. If neutrality requires that every group be in exactly the same position as every other, then neutrality appears impossible for, in the example quoted, whatever we do, someone is more favourably treated and therefore neutrality is not attained. Therefore, if the neutrality principle is to be of any practical use it must somehow, steer a course between the Scylla of sophistry and the Charybdis of incoherence.

Positive and negative neutrality

This distinction, also referred to earlier, concerns the amount and extent of activity required by the neutrality principle. In his Morrell Memorial Address Lord Scarman argues that 'standing back' is no longer sufficient for toleration. More is required by way of positive aid and assistance to those who would otherwise suffer disadvantage. The question there was 'does this mean that more than toleration is required in modern society, or does it mean that toleration involves more than merely letting alone?' A similar question may be posed here: is neutrality satisfied by negative considerations – not acting against people? Or is it rather the case that neutrality requires us to assist others? If the latter, then how much is necessary by way of assistance? Is equal opportunity enough, or does neutrality require that all flourish equally? Does it require equal fulfilment?

Putting all these points together, we generate the following problems about neutrality as a practical political policy:

1. The demand for neutrality presupposes that some clear and uncontroversial account can be given of the concept of harm, or of the distinction between the right and the good. This, however, is doubtful. There may be no such value-free account which can inform our decisions about neutrality.
2. Even if we assume that some line can be drawn between the right and the good (or between harm and offence), still our problems are not over, for we need to know whether neutrality as between competing conceptions of the good is satisfied by consideration of reasons only, or whether out-

comes must also be taken into account. Are we neutral if we simply refrain from aiming at the benefit of one group over another (if we desist from being non-neutral), or does neutrality refer to the consequences of our actions/omissions?
3. If the latter – i.e. if neutrality refers to outcomes, then how do we judge the success of a policy of neutrality? Is it required that all conceptions of the good should flourish equally, or is it required merely that all should have an equal opportunity of flourishing? And what is the criterion of equal opportunity independent of equal success? Is it possible to say that two individuals, or groups, have had equal opportunity despite the fact that they are not equally successful in pursuing their conceptions of the good?

In answer to the second question, it has already been noted that there are difficulties inherent in supposing neutrality to consist simply in neutrality with respect to reasons. Earlier, much was made of the invitation to sophistry which this conception of neutrality may imply. There is, however, another consideration which also militates against liberal employment of a conception of neutrality which has application only to reasons. The consideration is quite simply that such a conception can hardly be said to be characteristically liberal at all: in this minimalist form, all that the principle of neutrality denies is the legitimacy of assuming a single, correct conception of the good. In Lockean terms, it denies the propriety of attacking a religious belief simply because it is that religious belief. But neither socialist nor conservative political theories need depend for their justification upon a single specific conception of the good. Of course, they may do so, but they need not and insofar as that is true, a principle of neutrality with respect to reasons hardly serves to rule out very many alternatives to liberalism. In brief, liberal commitment to toleration is not distinguished by the reason-based version of neutrality. Thus, for example, Anne Phillips writes of socialists;

'if we hope to build solidarity on a firm foundation, we have to start from a clear understanding of the differences that divide us. Unity premissed on simple similarity can be powerful, but in the end restrictive – attractive, but in the end destructive.

We are not all the same, and the pretence that we are will not help us to change our world.' (Phillips, 1984, pp.239–40)

Similarly, writing of conservatism, Robert Nisbet remarks:

'In his indictment of Lord Hastings for his abuses of the Indian people and their customs Burke declared the Muslim and Hindu writs in India to be the equal in morality and humanity of Christianity. On an occasion when a group of Indians was visiting London and had been unable to win the assent of Anglican and Dissenter alike to brief use of a church for their own religious services, Burke extended the use of his house for this purpose.' (Nisbet, 1986, p.70)

There is, therefore, nothing quintessentially liberal about a doctrine of neutrality with respect to reasons. The reason for this is that, whilst many political doctrines may avoid foundation in a single conception of the good, liberalism is often characterised by its overt commitment to a plurality of goods. Given this commitment, it would be odd to rest content with a conception of neutrality which amounted to no more than the avoidance of non-neutrality. In order to arrive at something more distinctly liberal, therefore, the liberal must turn to a different account of neutrality – neutrality with respect to outcomes.

The requirements of neutrality

To flesh out the difficulties here, I shall return to the concept of neutrality invoked by Ronald Dworkin. Like Rawls, Dworkin rejects a minimalist, reason-based conception of neutrality in favour of a richer conception which makes reference to outcomes as well as to intentions. However, his reason for rejecting the minimalist account is not that it fails to isolate a distinctively liberal political order. Rather, he presents a characteristically liberal justification based upon the recognition of persons as entitled to equal concern and respect. This justification takes the form of a requirement that no laws should be passed or policies adopted which make it easier to pursue one conception of the good rather than another. In order to show equal concern and respect for all their citizens, governments must not pass laws the *consequences* of which are to make it easier to pursue one conception of the good rather than another. Where the reason-based argument precludes only actions *designed* to bring about disbenefit, this principle rules out actions which will *in fact* bring about disbenefit. Does this then mean that neutrality dictates equal fulfilment – that the neutrality requirement will be satisfied only when all conceptions of the good are equally realised? (Dworkin, 1985, pp.181–204.) Again Dworkin, like Rawls, resists this conclusion, urging a distinction between deserved and undeserved inequalities: different people may be more or less successful in pursuing their conceptions of the good. Where those inequalities in success are a consequence of individual preferences, then the costs of the preferences must be borne by the individuals themselves. If, for example, my conception of the good includes drinking champagne then (given the price of champagne) it is likely that I will be less successful in pursuing that conception than (say) beer drinkers will be in pursuing their conception. But my preference for champagne is just that – an expensive preference – and there is no reason why the state should subsidise my preference and impose the cost of it on those who choose to drink beer, or to be teetotal.

'Tastes as to which people differ are, by and large, not afflictions, like diseases, but are rather cultivated in accordance with each person's theory of what life should be like. The most effective neutrality, therefore, requires that the same share be devoted to each, so that the choice between expensive and less expensive tastes can be made by each person for himself, with no sense that his overall share will be enlarged by choosing a more expensive life, or that, whatever he chooses, his choice will subsidize those who have chosen more expensively.' (Dworkin, 1985, p.193)

So the conception of the good adopted by the champagne drinker will not necessarily be satisfied to the same extent as the conception of the good adopted by the beer drinker, or the teetotaller. The beer drinker and the champagne drinker are allocated equal shares and thus, we must presume, the high price of champagne will lead to less satisfaction for the champagne drinker than for the beer drinker. This, however, is not a violation of the principle of neutrality, since that principle requires only that all should have equal shares in order to pursue their conception of the good, not that all should have equal satisfaction or equal success in pursuing their conception of the good, however expensive it may be.

But of course not all inequalities are of this sort, and many, most notably the inequalities associated with physical handicap, are not chosen at all, but suffered: unlike the preference for champagne, they are not tastes or preferences, but conditions;

> 'some people will have special needs, because they are handicapped; their handicap will not only disable them from the most productive and lucrative employment, but will incapacitate them from using the proceeds of whatever employment they find as efficiently, so that they will need more than those who are not handicapped to satisfy identical ambitions.' (Dworkin, 1985, p.195).

We are not required to subsidise the expensive preferences and tastes of others, but we are required to subsidise or compensate for the unwanted inequalities suffered by others. On Dworkin's account, therefore, two related distinctions are employed: the distinction between what we choose and what we suffer; and the distinction between what we want and what we need. The requirement of neutrality, based upon equal concern and respect, demands that adjustments be made to accommodate needs which are suffered, but not preferences which are chosen. In brief, people must themselves bear the costs of their own expensive preferences but need not, indeed should not, be expected to bear the costs of unsought for and unwanted inequalities.

These distinctions dictate the form which neutrality will take in the liberal social order. The requirement that the state shall not make it easier to pursue one conception of the good rather than another is limited by the consideration that not all people begin in a position of equality with respect to their chances of pursuing their conception of the good. Where that inequality is, so to speak, undeserved, then the state must make allowance for that fact. By contrast, where the inequality is a consequence of choice, that is something which must be borne by the individual who does the choosing.

Two points emerge here which cast doubt upon the feasibility of proceeding as Dworkin wishes: firstly, the distinction between what is chosen and what is not chosen may often be more or less arbitrary: at the limit, of course, we can easily see that people do not choose physical handicap, and that they do choose (or cultivate) a taste for champagne. But other cases may be less straightforward. Conceptions of the good, as Dworkin himself points out, are not chosen in isolation, but by reference to the possibilities available. To repeat a point made in the previous chapter, we are victims as often as we are agents, and our decisions about the best way to live are often determined by the social and economic setting in which we find ourselves, rather than being the consequences of bare choice. Thus, for example, poverty and deprivation may set limits to our choices between ways of life just as effectively as does physical handicap. And similarly (though less often recognised) the 'choices' of the affluent are not always mere preferences which may be altered at a moment's notice. Choices are generated against the background of reasonable expectations, but that background is not itself chosen. It is given.

Secondly, and relatedly, Dworkin's enterprise relies heavily upon a distinction between what we want and what we need. But this is a quite separate distinction from the distinction between what we choose and what we suffer. In consequence, it is unclear whether the handicapped must be protected because they have not chosen to be handicapped, or because they need things which their handicap prevents them from getting. Moreover, there may be many cases in which the concept of need is itself under-determined: what we need may be a function of our conception of the good, rather than something separable from it. Since conceptions of the good are often not mere preferences, but the very things which give meaning to people's lives, being deprived of those things which are needed to pursue a conception of the good may be very serious indeed from a subjective point of view. In fact, it may be far more serious than physical handicap. Faced with a choice between physical disability and the unattainability of one's conception of the good, there is nothing irrational or incomprehensible about choosing the former.

Thus, on one interpretation, Dworkin's conception of neutrality depends upon a distinction between the chosen and the unchosen. Yet this, as was argued in the previous chapter, is a difficult distinction to sustain in practical cases. Moreover, reinterpreting the neutrality principle as founded upon a distinction between what we want and what we need will serve no better, for the correct analysis of needs, like the correct analysis of harm, is value-laden and not independent of conceptions of the good.

The consequence of this is that where neutrality is taken as requiring equal opportunity for all conceptions of the good, it will suffer from a double indeterminacy: there will be an initial indeterminacy of scope (it will be unclear where the line is to be drawn between the right and the good), and there will be a second indeterminacy in respect of what is chosen and what is not chosen; or what is wanted and what is needed. The neutrality principle will dictate different courses of action depending both on where we draw the line between what is chosen and what is not chosen, and on how we make the slightly different distinction between what is deemed to be a luxury and what a necessity. And there is enormous scope for disagreement in these areas, as may be seen by considering just one example used by Dworkin himself.

In his article 'Can a Liberal State Support Art?' Dworkin argues for state subsidy of the arts on the grounds that 'the choice between art and the rest is not a choice between luxury and necessity, grandeur and duty. We inherited a cultural structure, and we have some duty, out of simple justice, to leave that structure at least as rich as we found it' (Dworkin, 1985, p.233). But this implies that there is a substantial difference between preferences for champagne (which are not to be subsidised) and preferences for opera (which are). It implies, in fact, that the preference for art is not a mere preference after all, but something 'more lofty' – a necessity if our rich culture is to be sustained.

One problem with Dworkin's argument here is that it involves an equivocation on the word 'rich': if 'rich' is being employed quantitatively (to mean increasing choice), then a liberal defence of state subsidy of the arts looks plausible. The problem with this, however, is that that same argument would also imply the propriety of subsidising many other activities – football, roller-skating, hang-gliding. Subsidising these activities will make them available to a wider range of people, and will therefore increase choice. But Dworkin gives no hint of support for these. On the other hand, if 'rich' is understood qualitatively (to mean that opera is particularly valuable), then the neutrality principle is violated by state subsidy of the arts, for now the state does treat some conceptions of the good more favourably than others – it prefers opera lovers to football fans.

It is this latter, qualitative, interpretation which Dworkin presumably favours, for he refers to the arts not as luxuries but 'necessities'. Here again, however, the concept of need is evaluatively laden. If art really is a necessity, then it is a necessity which many (indeed most) people manage very well without. The truth is surely that this is a necessity only relative to the preservation of our culture, where 'our culture' does not even signify the culture of western democracies, but only, and at most, the culture of the educated middle classes of western democracies. Of course, there may be good reasons for preserving and sustaining that culture. But it seems unlikely that those reasons will have anything to do with justice or with the requirements of a principle of neutrality. Quite the reverse. It is a principle of partiality (of favouritism towards certain cultural interests) which dictates the practical policies advocated by Dworkin in this and other contexts.

Relatedly, we may wonder why it is that reference to the preservation of a rich culture is legitimate in arguments for the subsidy of the arts, but 'unhelpful' in arguments against the availability of pornography. In both cases claims are being made about the importance of sustaining or promoting a particular cultural environment. Why, then, should they be rejected when they are employed by feminists, but not when they are employed by opera lovers? It might be said that state subsidy of the arts will increase choice, whereas restriction on pornography will diminish choice, but again the feminist might reply in Dworkin's own terms – by pointing to the importance of sustaining a cultural environment which is, in some sense, rich. Moreover, many feminists claim, not implausibly, that something is lost by the proliferation of pornographic material. In so far as such material is construed as polluting our society, it does indeed destroy things of value: it destroys our cultural environment. Dworkin himself refers to this line of argument, but rejects it. It is not clear why he thinks that he is at liberty to reject it when it is employed as part of an attack on pornography, but equally at liberty to appeal to it as part of an argument for the state subsidy of art.

The charge against Dworkin appears, therefore, to be a charge not dissimilar to that levied against Mill: that neutrality ultimately manifests itself as cultural imperialism. Not, of course, in the sense that people are compelled to go to the opera, read Proust, or reject pushpin in favour of poetry. But only in the sense that the ideal subscribed to and promulgated by both Mill and Dworkin will favour these activities over other, less cerebral ones. Art lovers will find their conception of the good subsidised by Dworkin's liberal state: readers of comics must pay for their pleasures. And (adding insult to injury) feminists who oppose pornography are denied access to precisely the argument which Dworkin himself employs to justify subsidising the arts in the liberal state. Such principles may well issue in a state which is comfortable for the 'cultured' middle classes. It is difficult, however, to believe that it issues in a state which is neutral.

Personal and external preferences

It is necessary, at this stage, to introduce another distinction which Dworkin employs and which highlights yet further the evaluative basis from which his liberalism operates. The example of subsidy for the arts concentrated upon the difficulty of sustaining a value-free distinction between luxury and necessity. But this was only one distinction important to Dworkin, and to liberalism generally. The other distinction was between things which are chosen and things which are not chosen. Dworkin claims, to recall, that no special consideration is to be given to expensive tastes and preferences over cheap ones. People must bear the costs of their own expensive tastes. But the reverse side of this should be that all preferences count for the same. The requirement of equality is the requirement that we give equal resources, equal consideration, to all preferences. Dworkin recognises, however, that this principle may dictate undesirable social policies. Thus, for example, the preference of the white racist to live in a society purged of blacks will be given equal consideration with all others. To avoid this undesirable, and illiberal, conclusion he therefore makes a distinction between personal and external preferences, and argues that only the former may properly be taken into consideration in determining political policies.

The distinction between personal and external preferences is a distinction between preferences for one's own enjoyment of some goods or opportunities, and preferences for the assignment of goods and opportunities to others. The preference for champagne is personal – it concerns only what I want for myself. By contrast, the preference for an all-white society is ultimately an external preference.

'Consider the associational preference of a white law student for white classmates. This may be said to be a personal preference for an association with one kind of colleague rather than another. But it is a personal preference that is parasitic upon external preferences: except in very rare cases a white student prefers the company of other whites because he has racist social and political convictions, or because he has contempt for blacks as a group . . . it would be unfair to count preferences like these because these preferences make the success of the personal preferences depend upon the esteem and approval of others.' (Dworkin, 1977, p.236)

Thus, the principle of neutrality does not, after all, operate equally over all preferences. It distinguishes between personal preferences and external preferences. It must be neutral between preferences for champagne and preferences for beer, but need not (indeed should not) be neutral with respect to preferences for all-white communities. The latter are ruled out because, says Dworkin, they involve a denial of the principle of equal concern and respect. In so far as the requirement of neutrality is based upon the recognition that all people are entitled to equal concern and respect, it would be a violation, not an application of that principle to extend it to external preferences.

But again we may wonder how easy it is to draw an uncontroversial distinction between personal and external preferences. Dworkin claims that those who favour all-white societies are in fact evincing a contemptuous attitude towards blacks and, in the majority of cases, this is doubtless true. However, he has no *argument* against those who claim that their preference is simply that – a personal preference, just like the preference for champagne. Racists may always claim that, like champagne drinkers, they simply have a preference for a particular way of life; a preference about how they themselves live. Dworkin values the rich culture exemplified by opera. They value the cultural heritage manifest in all-English schools. Like Dworkin, we may not believe them, but neither does the distinction between personal and external preferences provide an argument against them.

Against this claim it might be pointed out that such preferences cannot count as purely personal, since they have implications for the ordering of society. If the racist's preference for living in an all-white society is to be satisfied, then burdens and restrictions must be imposed upon others – specifically, upon blacks. The supposedly personal preferences of racists cannot in fact be construed as personal, since they extend beyond themselves and have consequences for others. This, however, is an unpromising line of argument. On inspection, there are very few preferences which are not of this sort. We may say against Dworkin, as many have said against Mill, that the distinction between the personal and the external, like the distinction between the self-regarding and the other-regarding, is largely untenable. All but the most trivial and insignificant of my preferences have consequences for others. My personal preference for smoking cigarettes, for example, has clear consequences for others, who themselves have a personal preference for a smoke-free environment. My preference for reading pornographic literature in the privacy of my own home has consequences for others, since if that preference is to be satisfied, such literature must be on sale. There must be an industry which produces and disseminates it. There must be women willing to participate in the production of it. There must be booksellers and newsagents able to make it available to those who want it.

The implications of these considerations for questions of toleration should, by now, be fairly clear: if the neutrality principle sets limits to what may properly be tolerated, then it stands in need of clarification. However, attempts to clarify the distinctions between the chosen and the unchosen; between luxury and necessity; and between personal and external preferences, were all fraught with difficulty. If these distinctions are difficult to draw, then the limits of toleration will be equally difficult to draw.

Moreover, even assuming that the distinctions can be drawn, it is not obvious that Dworkin draws and applies them consistently. Thus, for example, he defends the right of the anti-Vietnam protestor to shout obscenities, but denies that there is any right to expose oneself in the park. Why? The Vietnam example is an example of someone agitating on behalf of an external preference, whereas indecent exposure may well be just a personal preference for leading one's life in a certain way. Relatedly, it may well be misleading to describe the penchant for exposing oneself as a 'preference' at all: it is, perhaps, not something chosen, but an unalterable feature of one's nature, far less malleable in many respects than a political principle. Why should it not be tolerated? The irresistible conclusion is that Dworkin's principle is not a principle of neutrality after all, but a principle informed by a highly intellectual theory of human nature.

> 'Dworkin assumes that we all share roughly the same scale of values as he does; that we rank anti-draft demonstrations above old ladies' feelings, but have little regard for the rights of flashers . . . he appeals to the liberal model of the self-developing rational chooser of ends characteristic of the rationalist tradition of Kant and Mill. It is this conception of human agency which does the real work in his theory, allowing him to rank the rights of the individualist above those of the conformist.' (Bellamy, 1988)

Conclusion

What are the conclusions to be drawn from the preceding discussion of neutrality as the guiding political aim of liberalism? In particular, what are the consequences for toleration in the liberal social order? Three theories of neutrality have been considered.

The first was the Lockean theory, according to which neutrality demands only that we should avoid certain reasons for intolerance. We are neutral in so far as we do not aim at or intend to attack certain conceptions of the good. This principle, however, invites sophistry, and a society based on it might be quite intolerant in its observable characteristics, even if not in its professed aims. It might, for example, be indifferent about the plight of minorities who need positive aid and assistance if their conception of the good is not to wither away and die. Moreover, this conception of neutrality is not the one which should commend itself to liberals, since it fails to justify a characteristically liberal social order. It is an interpretation of neutrality equally available to writers from other political traditions.

In response to these difficulties, a second account of neutrality was proposed which concerns itself with outcomes rather than with reasons. There are, broadly speaking, two ways in which neutrality in respect of outcomes can be required: it may be thought that neutrality demands equal fulfilment of all conceptions of the good, or it may be thought simply that neutrality demands equal respect for all conceptions of the good. The former analysis did not detain us long, for it was fairly clear that such a conception would turn out to be unrealisable both in principle and in practice.

The latter therefore constituted the most plausible alternative to the reason-based interpretation, and in this context Ronald Dworkin's account was taken as representative, though it is an account many of whose main features are shared by other liberals, including John Rawls.

Dworkin's account construes neutrality as flowing from considerations of equal respect and concern. It requires that the liberal state shall be neutral in the sense that it does not make it easier to pursue one conception of the good rather than another. (Note that this is not the positive claim that the state shall actively promote all conceptions of the good equally. It is merely the negative claim that the state shall refrain from doing anything whose consequences are to favour one conception of the good over another. Thus, this version of the neutrality principle is also a principle of restraint.) However, this account of neutrality was problematic in a variety of ways: it depends upon a distinction between deserved and undeserved inequalities and upon a related distinction between wants and needs or between luxuries and necessities. These, it was suggested, are highly contentious distinctions and ones which may serve to render the neutrality principle unworkable.

Moreover, its consequences for questions of toleration are highly controversial. Thus, for example, Dworkin employs the principle in arguments which purport to show both that anti-Vietnam demonstrators have a right to use obscene language in demonstrating for their cause, and that there is no right to engage in displays of public indecency (exposing oneself in the park, for example). It is far from clear why the principle of equality delivers such conclusions, and even less clear that what it delivers is neutral between competing conceptions of the good. Of course, and as Dworkin rightly points out, he is not committed to being neutral about neutrality. He need not, for example, defend those forms of expression which would undermine the principle of equality itself. So he need not defend the Nazi's right to promote racist legislation. But that still leaves quite considerable room for anti-social activities and, again, it is not obvious why some of these should be tolerated and others not.

Thus, the three interpretations of neutrality are all fraught with difficulty and the only one which delivers clear and consistent practical advice about how the state should conduct itself is the reason-based conception favoured by Locke. This conception, however, was precisely the one thought to be least helpful to liberalism. Unlike the others, it is not a conception which captures the spirit of the liberal approach to politics.

The conclusion of this chapter is therefore that liberals are faced with a stark choice: in practical politics, they must either adopt a reason-based conception of neutrality, in which case their theory will be consistent, but not characteristically liberal. Or they must adopt a more extensive conception of neutrality, in which case their theory will be liberal, but not consistent. Most importantly, in questions of toleration they will (in practice) favour some conceptions of the good over others. The indifference of a Lockean conception of neutrality may be avoided, but the price is high. When such a conception is abandoned it is replaced by conceptions which, ultimately, are not neutral at all, but partial, and which show scant regard for non-individualist, non-intellectual conceptions of the good.

Finally, I wish to draw attention to the differences between the conclusions of this chapter and the conclusions of the previous chapter. In so far as Chapter 4 was concerned with the conceptual foundations of liberalism, and in particular with its foundation in autonomy, it alleged that liberalism could do no more than construe the toleration of non-autonomy valuing sub-groups as a necessary evil, not a genuine good. In so far as this chapter has been concerned with the practical policies implemented in the liberal state, it argues that for many liberals toleration will not extend even this far. Neither autonomy, as the conceptual foundation of liberalism, nor neutrality, as the guiding political vision of liberalism, can effectively guarantee a society which is truly diverse, plural and tolerant.

In the final section I shall draw together the threads of the arguments of this book, and ask how much we can reasonably expect of a theory of toleration.

6 Choice, Community and Socialism

'If you prick us, do we not bleed?' (*Merchant of Venice*)

The arguments of this book have considered the historical and conceptual foundations of toleration in liberal political theory. At the outset, three central questions were isolated: 'What is toleration?' 'What is the justification of toleration?' and 'What are the limits of toleration?' A distinction was drawn between the defence of toleration offered by Locke in his *Letter on Toleration* and the defence offered by Mill in *On Liberty*. Locke's narrower and more pragmatic account is often unfavourably compared with Mill's doctrine and it is frequently urged that whilst Mill captures the spirit of the liberal approach to politics, Locke's account is philosophically dead. The arguments of the preceding chapters should, however, give us cause to wonder whether this is a fair assessment.

In discussing Locke's account, I noted that it is often thought to be flawed in three ways: it is an account which emphasises the irrationality of intolerance, not its immorality; it concentrates on the illegitimacy of specific reasons for intolerance, but says little about its consequences; and it focuses on the duties of would-be perpetrators of intolerance, not on the wrong done to its victims. In each of these three respects, it is suggested, Locke's account is inadequate and should give way to the more richly liberal account offered by Mill.

By contrast with Locke, Mill embeds his defence of toleration in a more general defence of the positive value of liberty, which is held to be important because of its role in promoting and fostering autonomy. Without liberty, the rich variety of human nature will degenerate into numbing uniformity, and individuals will be

oppressed not only by intolerant laws but also, and most importantly, by intolerant social attitudes. It is, therefore, the crucial role
of liberty in fostering and promoting autonomy which generates a
requirement of toleration in Mill's work. Moreover, this defence
is the one which has been most influential in modern liberal
accounts of toleration.

Putting these points together delivers a consensus in favour of
Mill's approach to the problems: in answer to the question 'What
is the justification of toleration?' or 'Why is toleration thought to
be a good?' Mill can reply that its justification lies not in the
historically specific features of nineteenth-century British and
European society, but rather in quite general considerations
about human nature and individual autonomy. The diversity of
individuals, their need to flourish and grow, dictates the necessity
of toleration. Similarly, in response to the question 'What are the
limits of toleration?' Mill may reply that it is limited also by
considerations of autonomy. Toleration is not required in circumstances in which it will be employed so as to stifle and stunt the
growth of autonomous individuality.

Locke, on the other hand, presents a much more restricted case
for toleration than does Mill: he has no positive argument for the
good of toleration as such but only, and at best, a negative
argument against the irrationality of persecution. His case is
historically specific in that it considers only the toleration of
varieties of Christian belief, and aims to show why the refusal of
toleration to those varieties is irrational, not why it is morally
wrong. Thus, in answer to the question 'What is the justification
of toleration?' Locke gives no completely general answer: his
justification is a justification of religious toleration and, even within
that restricted sphere, his claim is not that it is a good, but that it
is a rational requirement.

So much is standard interpretation of the defences of toleration
found in Locke and Mill. However, in the chapter on Locke I
suggested that his account does contain something philosophically
alive and valuable – that it deserves more attention than is usually
paid to it. Moreover, subsequent chapters have served to cast
doubt upon the plausibility of more extensive, autonomy-based
defences which are found in Mill and developed by modern
liberals. The implication of these two lines of thought is to suggest
that liberal defences of toleration should adopt the reason-based

form advocated by Locke and give up their more ambitious claims. This may seem a depressing, even a defeatist, conclusion: the dream of the neutral state in which all might flourish and develop autonomy has been renounced in favour simply of a set of guidelines for legislators. The situation is not, however, as gloomy as it may at first appear, for the pragmatic considerations adduced by Locke may provide the basis for a more extensive, socialist defence of toleration. In this final chapter I shall attempt to draw together the threads of the argument and to indicate the moral importance of such an approach.

The main highways to toleration

At the outset, three ways of justifying toleration were noted and discussed. These were: the argument from scepticism, the argument from neutrality, and the argument from autonomy. The three defences of toleration were also presented as possible defences of liberalism. Liberalism may be based on scepticism (the denial that there is any such thing as moral or religious truth); it may be based on the aspiration to neutrality (the belief that the state should not favour one conception of the good over another); or it may be based on autonomy (the belief that each person ought to be allowed to lead his own life in his own way). Underpinning these three justifications of liberalism and of toleration was a fundamental commitment to ι   ιiberalism, it was said, begins from a premise of individual diversity: each person has his own unique conception of what makes life worth living and is entitled to pursue that conception to the best of his ability. If liberalism is premised on the fact of diversity, then it is comparatively easy to see why the need for toleration will arise. Amongst the many and diverse forms of life within society, some will be found repellent. Some will conflict with others. Some will be thought morally wrong. Toleration will therefore be a pragmatic necessity if civil peace and harmony are to be maintained. It will also be morally required in the interests of individual autonomy.

Yet diversity has not been the only, nor the most significant, feature of modern liberalism and its defences of toleration. Two other concepts have been equally powerful and pervasive. These are the concepts of choice and of rationality or transparency.

Choice

In rejecting the attempt to found liberalism on moral scepticism, Ronald Dworkin claims that scepticism is precisely the wrong answer to make in response to questions about toleration. He says; 'if the moral majority is wrong, and each person should be free to choose personal ideals for himself, then this is surely because the choice of one sort of life over another is a matter of supreme importance, not because it is of no importance at all' (Dworkin, 1983, p.47).

Contrast this statement with another, also referred to earlier;

'There are points of resemblance between moral and factual convictions; and I suspect it to be true of moral, as it certainly is of factual convictions, that we cannot take very seriously a profession of them if we are given to understand that a speaker has just decided to adopt them . . . We see a man's genuine convictions as coming from somewhere deeper in him than that.' (Williams, 1973, p.227)

The belief in autonomy and the requirement of neutrality both imply that ways of life, commitments, moral ideals, are at root matters of individual choice. Political toleration is then a necessity if such choice is to be fostered. It is, as we have seen, not merely belief in diversity, but the desirability of 'making one's own life' which generates the liberal commitment to toleration. Yet we may wonder, with Williams, whether it is in fact true that the 'supremely important' features of our lives are matters of choice. Part of the argument of Chapter 4 was intended to raise this very question and to suggest that the room for choice of personal ideal is much more restricted than liberals assume. Moreover, choice is arguably inapplicable in some of the central cases of toleration mentioned earlier.

The very first example of toleration discussed in this book was racial toleration, and I mentioned there the fact that there is a slight oddity in speaking of toleration in a racial context. One reason for the oddity is that toleration implies that the thing tolerated is morally reprehensible. Another is the implication that it is alterable. To speak of tolerating another implies that it is to his discredit that he does not change that feature of himself which is the object of toleration. (Hence Mary Warnock may properly claim to tolerate her son-in-law when he wears sandals with a suit.) But that implication is false in the racial case: there is nothing morally reprehensible about belonging to a different race or being of a different colour. Nor is there anything the agent can do to change that feature of himself. Cultural identity is malleable, but racial identity is not. To the extent that this is so, reference to 'racial tolerance' may be somewhat misleading.

Similar points can be made about religious toleration and sexual toleration. Whatever might be said about the moral repugnance of homosexuality, about the deep-rooted belief that homosexuality is 'at best an inferior way of life' and 'at worst a sickening perversion', it is also important to bear in mind that we have very little control over or choice about our sexual preferences. To this extent, talk of sexual 'preferences' is itself misleading.

And the same point applies to deeply-held moral or religious belief. Phillips and Mounce express something like this thought in the story they tell of a Roman Catholic mother reluctant to agree to the use of contraceptives. However much her G.P. might try to persuade her that contraception will enhance her quality of life, she does not believe that that is so. The doctor is working on the assumption that moral beliefs are a function of desires, and that desires are rational in so far as they promote our interests. Once the woman has been persuaded to see that her desires are not in her best interests, nor in the best interests of society as a whole, she will revise her moral beliefs accordingly. But, as Phillips and Mounce put it, 'the mother does not believe because she wants. She wants because she believes.' Her moral beliefs dictate her desires. And she cannot therefore choose or decide what she wants. What she wants, and what she takes to be in her interests, flows from the framework of moral and religious beliefs within which she stands. For her, there is no supremely important choice between ways of life, but only a recognition of the terms within which her life is conducted.

What consequences do these considerations have for questions of toleration? At first glance it might appear that the scope for toleration is seriously restricted by reflection on the unalterability of our lives. If toleration can correctly be applied only to what is alterable, and if many of the most important features of our lives are not alterable (not the object of choice or of decision), then toleration becomes diminishingly important. At the limit, its scope will be restricted to the choice of whether to wear sandals with a suit. Again, this may appear a depressing conclusion for those anxious to defend the value of toleration. What began as a central value of political life has become merely a side-show for dealing with the comparatively trivial. But I shall return to choice and alterability later, and try to use them to provide a more optimistic analysis of the role of toleration in modern society.

Rationality

The second central feature of liberalism is rationality. In a recent article, 'Theoretical Foundations of Liberalism', Jeremy Waldron says;

> 'The view that I want to identify as a foundation of liberal thought is based on this demand for a justification of the social world. Like his empiricist counterparts in science, the liberal insists that intelligible justifications in social and political life must be available in principle for everyone, for society is to be understood by the human mind, not by the tradition or sense of a community.' (Waldron, 1987, p.135)

This requirement he calls the requirement of transparency;

> 'Society should be a *transparent* order, in the sense that its workings and principles should be well-known and available for public apprehension and scrutiny. People should know and understand the reasons for the basic distribution of wealth, power, authority, and freedom. Society should not be shrouded in mystery, and its workings should not have to depend on mythology, mystification or "the noble lie".' (p.146)

The requirement of transparency certainly implies rationality. But it need not, strictly speaking, imply rationalism. It implies that social institutions and orders must not rest upon deceit and error – on mystification, mythology and the noble lie. But it need not insist that everything shall be totally explicable. This latter, however, is often the conclusion which liberals do in fact reach.

Indeed, Waldron himself (correctly) identifies the home and the family as places where important issues of power arise, and he claims that if liberals refuse to recognise this they will 'leave themselves open to the charge of being less than whole-hearted about the legitimation of all structures of power in modern society' (p.147). The overwhelming impression left by commitment to choice and to rationality is an impression of the world as a supermarket, where prices must be clearly labelled and contents exhaustively described. The discriminating shopper has a right to know what is in the tin.

Again, we may ask, 'What are the implications of this for the theory of toleration?' It was suggested earlier that room for toleration diminishes if we believe (with Williams) that the most important and valuable features of our lives are not matters for choice. Similarly here, room for political toleration diminishes if we believe that many of the most important structures of our lives are not proper objects of legitimation: if, that is to say, we believe that although these structures should not depend on deception, they are nevertheless not susceptible to complete and rational explanation. Again, for contrast, compare the quotation from Waldron with the following;

'It is one aspiration, that social and ethical relations should not essentially rest on ignorance and misunderstanding of what they are, and quite another that all the beliefs and principles involved in them should be explicitly stated. That these are two different things is obvious with personal relations, where to hope that they do not rest on deceit and error is merely decent, but to think that their basis can be made totally explicit is idiocy.' (Williams, 1985, p.102)

Requirements of transparency, or of rationality, lead so far and no further. In so far as the liberal scheme of things is premised upon the need for transparency it will, of necessity, leave much unexplained. This is not simply because there are areas of 'private' life, in which the state has no business. So much is commonplace in liberal thought – indeed, insistence on the public–private distinction is itself characteristic of much liberal thought. Rather, the point is that these 'private' areas do not lend themselves to the necessary legitimation process. It is not, as the liberal often implies, that they *should not* be legitimised, but that they *cannot* be legitimised in the appropriate sense. Hence the dilemma which Waldron isolates: if liberalism insists on the legitimation of all structures of power within society, then liberalism must insist on the legitimation of domestic relationships, since they are important power structures. The drive to rationality or transparency is the drive to interpret everything on the model of the public.

The example of marriage is instructive here: the complaints of liberal feminists about the marriage relationship have frequently taken the form of objections to the unfairness inherent in the terms of the contract. What liberals, from Mill and William Thompson onwards, have demanded is that those terms should be made fairer – they should be such that it is possible rationally to agree to them. Liberals have rarely objected to the claim that marriage is a contractual relationship. Yet we may wonder whether this is an appropriate way of looking at things: 'The social conditions within which human beings can develop and flourish are formed by the non-contractual relationships that contractarianism attempts to eliminate. There is no place for love within the standpoint of contract unless, that is, it is reduced to no more than sexual inclination and satisfaction' (Pateman, 1984, pp.89–90; see also Pateman, 1988). The requirement of legitimation is a requirement which generates the contractarian view, since contract is one very obvious way in which arrangements may be made transparent. Here too liberalism tends to interpret everything on the supermarket model. There is an insistence that we should be sure of getting value for money, or a fair deal, or consumer rights.

These reflections on the importance of choice and of legitimation have two consequences for questions of toleration: liberals exaggerate the extent to which choice is possible in the case of personal ideals, and thus exaggerate the scope of toleration. Similarly, liberals exaggerate the extent to which legitimation is appropriate in the case of our most deeply held relationships, and thus exaggerate the importance of toleration. Toleration may be a central virtue of a liberal society, but it can be that only on the assumption that many features of our lives are alterable and many features of our lives are appropriate objects of legitimation.

How, then, should we understand toleration, its justification and its limits in modern society? The burden of my negative points against liberalism, both here and in the earlier chapters, has been to suggest that there is, after all, no 'brave, naked will'. We are, I have claimed, passive as well as active; victims as well as agents. Within lives, the choice of personal ideals is not genuinely a choice at all. Between lives, the legitimation of structures of power is most appropriate in business or professional relationships, not in relationships of a more personal sort. Thus, in many of the areas which are most important to people, the liberal conception of toleration has a diminishingly important role. What are the alternative ways of understanding toleration and its role in society? I shall consider just one set of possibilities, the role of toleration in socialism. Here, it seems to me, there are the seeds of a richer, yet more disturbing concept of toleration than is found within liberalism. The socialist perspective can give us a better understanding of why toleration is valuable, but it will not ascribe to toleration the central position which the liberalism advocates. Toleration – even extensive toleration – is not enough in the socialist scheme of things.

Toleration in socialism

There is no reason to believe that socialism, or conservatism, will be any more amenable to clear and uncontroversial definition than was liberalism. However, one important difference between socialism and liberalism lies in their differing conceptions of the relationship between individual and society. This much, at least, is true: socialists do not see the state as merely a neutral arena in which people may pursue their own interests and personal projects unhampered by others. In socialism;

> 'each member of society should ideally see himself as bound to the other members in such a way that he feels himself responsible for their welfare. In addition, his identity is at least partially constituted by his social membership; in answer to the question "Who are you?", he says, among other things, "I belong to . . .".' (Miller, 1988, p.240)

This conception of the role of the individual in society reflects the fact that many features of our lives are given (they are not objects of choice). But it also reflects the socialist belief that the state is

more influential and all-pervasive than liberals claim: if the state
can provide an important sense of citizenship, if it can invest
people's lives with meaning, and give them a sense of belonging,
then it must be more than the supermarket of individual choice.
At one and the same time this dictates both more and less extensive
toleration. As David Miller has argued, the sense of common
citizenship required by socialism appears to dictate diminishing
toleration of sub-groups which demand loyalty at odds with loyalty
to the overall community. 'Subcultures threaten to undermine the
overarching sense of identity that socialism requires. They are
liable to do so in two ways: they give participants a narrower focus
of loyalty that may pre-empt commitment to the wider community;
and by way of reaction people outside a particular subculture may
find it difficult to identify with those who are seen as in some way
separated off' (Miller, 1988, p.244). The subversive aspects of
subcultures within a wider socialist, community thus leads in the
direction of limited toleration. Indeed, it raises the spectre of
totalitarianism which Berlin finds so threatening, for it implies that
there is a single right way of belonging, a single truth about the
best way to live. At the same time, however, socialism may also
dictate extended toleration: the reasons for this are two-fold.

First, the consideration that people are victims as much as
agents, that often they simply belong, and do not *choose* to belong
to the subculture or sub-group in which they find themselves,
dictates practical policies of toleration. If what is important is that
people should have a sense of belonging to the wider community,
as well as belonging to the subculture, then that is not something
which can be foisted upon them by legislative dictate. Like religious
belief, membership is something we acknowledge, not something
we can be coerced into accepting. Political intolerance would
therefore be irrational in such cases, for it would attempt to employ
'force and blood', 'rods and axes', 'fire and the sword' to change
men's beliefs and commitments. This practical point is, of course,
one which has its origins in Locke. It is far from being a specifically
socialist reason in favour of toleration. If we are to adduce socialist
justifications of toleration we must do more than point to the
irrationality of intolerance.

Secondly, therefore, we must ask whether socialism can do more
than advocate toleration as a pragmatic device or temporary
expedient. In criticising autonomy-based liberalism I argued that,

too often, it would extend toleration only as a pragmatic device against the great day when all become autonomous. There is a hint of this in Joseph Raz's claim that 'for those who live in an autonomy-supporting environment there is no choice but to be autonomous' and that therefore members of subcultures must be brought 'humanely and decently' to placing value on the condition of autonomy (Raz, 1986, p.391). Can socialists do any better than this? The prognosis is not good: socialists have been just as prone as liberals to construe loyalty to a subculture as a piece of false consciousness which will miraculously disappear with the coming of the socialist state. Yet such an understanding of ethnic identity is not a necessary part of socialist ideology (though it is often thought to be so). This brings us to the second, more principled, way in which socialists may offer extended toleration.

Earlier in the book, I quoted Anne Phillips' warning to socialists;

> 'we should not act as if the only solidarity worth its name is the one that unites through every aspect of our existence. Rather, we should think of socialist unity as a complicated – maybe even painful – construction from many *different* solidarities, some of which will inevitably be in conflict.' (Phillips, 1984, pp.240–1)

The development of Britain and America as multi-cultural and multi-racial societies gives prominence to difficulties inherent in socialist conceptions of solidarity and citizenship. Why should socialists extend toleration to subcultures whose narrower loyalties threaten to subvert the wider (and grander) aim of building a socialist society? There is, of course, the pragmatic reason already referred to: we cannot coerce a sense of solidarity or of citizenship, and it is therefore irrational to attempt to do so by means of the legislative equipment at the disposal of the state.

Anne Phillips' argument, however, supplements the pragmatic consideration with a moral one. If socialism emphasises the importance of the 'given' and of the interdependence between people, if, that is to say, it sees a sense of belonging as being of crucial importance, then this will provide a new justification of toleration, and one not readily available to liberalism. Socialist unity, according to Phillips, must be construed not as a single solidarity, but as a construction from many different solidarities. The problem of construction is acute in multi-cultural and multi-racial societies, where loyalty to the subculture may conflict with loyalty to the overarching state. Nevertheless, it is a problem which also occurs outside of multi-cultural societies. As we have already seen, it is implicit in the homosexual community's declaration 'WE ARE GOING TO BE WHO WE ARE'. It is also implicit in much feminist discontent with modern society, for the language of socialist solidarity has traditionally been the language of fraternity. Such language, by implication, advocates a solidarity premised on exclusion, 'a unity derived from a womanless world'. The demand for a *construction* of socialist unity from different solidarities is thus, in itself, a demand for toleration. It is the articulation of a desire to belong to the wider community, but to belong one one's own terms, without taking on wholesale the values of the wider community. It is, in part, the demand made by Shylock. If Phillips is right, then toleration is a moral necessity of a socialist society, not just a requirement of expediency.

Most importantly, this understanding of the need for toleration answers more honestly to the complaints of those who feel that too much is being tolerated in society, or that not enough is tolerated. There is indeed no algorithm which dictates the precise policies of toleration which should operate in society, and this will be just as true of socialist societies as it is of liberal ones.

Nevertheless, there can be better or worse explanations of what wrong is done when individuals, or groups feel the policies of the state to be misguided. In discussing feminist objections to the availability of pornography, I made reference to Andrea Dworkin's claim 'pornography is violence against women', and to Ronald Dworkin's counter-claim that a permissive attitude to pornography is required if the right of moral independence is not to be violated. I noted there that the perspective of rights may result in insoluble conflict: from the point of view of the consumer of pornography, moral independence is threatened by restriction; from the point of view of the opponent of pornography, moral independence is threatened by permission.

Yet the real problem is not the restriction on freedom which may result from too tolerant or too intolerant an attitude. The feminist does not, at root, complain that her moral independence is threatened by the knowledge that others are consuming pornography in private. Nor need she, in any straightforward way, claim that pornography is culturally polluting (though she may claim this). Rather, her claim may be that she is alienated from a society which thinks of the matter in these terms. It is impossible for her to feel any sense of belonging or of loyalty to a state which uses her sexuality in this way. And similar points may be made in other areas. Homosexuals need not feel that their moral independence is threatened by the attitudes of others. They may rather feel that they cannot identify with a state which simply refrains from using its coercive power against them. 'WE ARE GOING TO BE WHO WE ARE' can be construed either as a defiant challenge to a state which would coerce, or (more worryingly) as an expression of profound alienation from that state.

Although these arguments are presented as ones which indicate the moral role of toleration in a socialist society, they also point in a different direction: socialists, unlike liberals, do not see the state as a neutral arena. They require that members of the society should see themselves as bound to it and to each other by bonds of common citizenship. They aspire to promote a sense of loyalty and of belonging amongst members of the state. In so far as this is so, they require both more and less toleration than do liberals. More, because toleration is a necessary component of the development of a larger loyalty. Less, because toleration will not, on its own, be enough to instil the requisite sense of belonging. If I am to feel that I belong, I must also feel that more than toleration is being extended to me. I must feel that others respect and esteem me, not that they simply put up with me.

Thus, the sectarian loyalties of minorities must somehow be accommodated within the overarching sense of socialist citizenship. Their sense of belonging to the smaller group must be converted into a larger loyalty to the state as a whole. Socialist society 'must try to present an interpretation of, let us say, Indian culture in Britain, that makes it possible for members of the Indian community to feel at home in and loyal to, the British state' (Miller, 1988, p.153). At the same time, of course, the state itself must refrain from insisting upon any simple solidarity. Again, 'we should think of socialist unity as a complicated – maybe even a painful – construction from many *different* solidarities, some of which will inevitably be in conflict'.

At the beginning of this book I quoted Lord Scarman's claim that toleration today requires more than the absence of impediment or discrimination under the law; 'Man today requires more of the law than that he be left alone to pursue his way of life as he sees fit. Today he asks of the law positive rights enforceable against the state, against his employer, and indeed on occasions against the rest of us' (Scarman, 1987, p.54). I asked whether this meant that man requires more than toleration, and my conclusion is that, in a sense, he does.

If the circumstances of toleration are circumstances of diversity coupled with dislike, disapproval or disgust, then tolerating means putting up with things which we dislike, disapprove of, or find disgusting. Why should this be required, and why should more than this be required? What are the grounds for offering even this, and what are the limits of it? I have argued that in liberalism the grounds of toleration are to be found in the requirement that the state shall be neutral, and the limits of toleration are to be found by appeal to the concept of autonomy. If this, liberal, interpretation is correct, then Lord Scarman does not ask for more than toleration. The requirement of state neutrality and the need to foster autonomy may themselves dictate extensive state action to neutralise the effects of social and economic disadvantage: positive discrimination and affirmative action will be the mechanisms by which the state counters individual and social prejudice. Official and extensive toleration will be the antidote to individual intolerance.

Yet the real damage done both by toleration and by intolerance is precisely the same. When people are the recipients of state toleration, they may feel as much alienated from the wider society as they do when they are persecuted. The need which is felt by persecuted minorities is not a need which can be satisfied by liberal toleration – however extensive it may be. Such people demand respect, and esteem. They want to be welcomed and wanted. They want to feel that they belong. It is this need to belong which is addressed by the socialist account of toleration, and it is important to recognise the great differences which divide it from the liberal account. To emphasise this, I shall conclude by pointing to the different answers which liberalism and socialism give to questions about the justification and limits of toleration, as well as to the resolution of the paradox of toleration.

In response to the question 'What justifies toleration?' liberals will refer to the importance of freedom of choice and individual autonomy. It is the importance of leading one's own life in one's own way which provides the rationale for a policy of toleration. People must be free to choose their own personal ideas. By contrast, socialists will justify toleration both as a way of promoting a sense of citizenship, and as a way of sustaining a sense of citizenship. It is not merely the liberal belief that we are not all the same which generates socialist commitment to toleration. It is also the socialist desire to create a society where all can feel that they belong. Moreover, the difficulty of promoting this sense of belonging is generated precisely because we do not, as the liberal supposes, choose our personal ideals on an individual basis. If we did, then toleration would be only a temporary expedient against the day when members of subcultures choose better or more rationally. But we are not either, as the conservative imagines, locked in an historically given identity. If our identity were not malleable there would be no point in toleration. The combination of a given, yet malleable, identity creates the need for and justification of toleration. A distinction needs to be made between that which is an object of individual decision or choice and that which is alterable. The liberal believes that personal ideals are both alterable and matters of choice. He thus, ultimately, sees toleration as pragmatic. The conservative sees personal ideals as neither chosen nor alterable. He thus sees toleration as necessary only if it will avert a greater disaster. The socialist, by contrast, sees personal ideals as alterable, but not the objects of choice. He therefore sees toleration as practically necessary, but also as morally required in the construction of a complex sense of socialist unity. What, then, are the limits of toleration?

In response to this question, the liberal claims that the justification of toleration also provides its limits: we should tolerate all and only those actions which do not constitute an infringement of autonomy. If toleration is justified by the consideration that people have a right to lead their own lives in their own way, then it is equally limited by that same consideration. For the socialist, however, the situation is more complex and, potentially, more sinister in its implications. If toleration is justified because it is a way of promoting a sense of belonging, then there can be no justification for tolerating those actions or beliefs which do not promote a sense of belonging. The ground is ripe for widespread suppression of those loyalties which conflict with the larger loyalty to society as a whole, and the only reason the socialist will have for refraining from such actions is the purely pragmatic one that, in fact, and in some cases, suppression will merely serve to increase alienation. The limits of toleration appear here to be very tightly drawn. Again, however, these limits are tightly drawn only on the assumption that socialist solidarity is a monolithic notion. Only, that is to say, on the assumption that socialist unity will not be a construction of many different solidarities.

In these respects, however, it may be said that the liberal is not, theoretically, any worse off than the socialist. Just as the limits of socialist toleration need not be restrictive, so the limits of liberal toleration need not be restrictive. The argument that liberalism did not promote a genuinely plural and tolerant society was valid only on the assumption that non-autonomy-valuing life styles would be many rather than few in number. Similarly here, the argument that socialism will not prove unduly restrictive in what it tolerates is valid only on the assumption that the different solidarities will be many rather than few in number. This criticism may be well-founded and perhaps it would not be wholly surprising if it were: socialism has its historical roots in liberalism, and the forms of argument employed in the one will not be completely alien to the other.

Finally, however, I wish to address again the paradox of toleration, for it is here, I think, that the socialist does have a distinctive, and superior, response. The paradox, to recall, is why it can be right to tolerate that which we believe to be wrong.

'To disapprove of something is to judge it to be wrong. Such a judgement does not express a purely subjective preference. It claims universality; it claims to be the view of any rational agent. The content of the judgement that something is wrong, implies that the something may properly be prevented. But if your judgement is reasonably grounded, why should you go against it at all? Why should you tolerate?' (Raphael, 1988, p.139)

In the liberal scheme of things the answer to this question is (often) that toleration implies respect for persons as autonomous agents. It is the need to respect that autonomy which solves the paradox of toleration: we ought to tolerate what is morally wrong because it is part of being an autonomous agent that one should be allowed to do what is morally wrong. Again, the guiding picture is of the state as a neutral arena for facilitating the choices which people make. But the socialist conception places far less emphasis on choice. It construes people's ideals as malleable, but nevertheless given. As alterable, but nevertheless not the objects of choice or decision. Against this background, persecution would be inappropriate. People do not choose their ideals in any straightforward way, nor can they choose to renounce the ideals, however morally repugnant others might find them. It is, therefore, at least partly because choice is inappropriate that socialists will recommend practical policies of toleration. But this, as we have seen, is not enough for a specifically socialist answer to the problem.

What generates a socialist response to the problem is a further thought about the precise nature of the wrong done to people if they are not tolerated. The wrong is not to be explained by reference to loss of moral independence, or denial of autonomy, but by reference to the feeling of separateness and distance between the individual and the overarching society. We should tolerate – and more than tolerate – if we expect to create a society in which people can identify their good with the good of others, and come to feel that they speak through their society and that it speaks for them. What the socialist conception points to is a different understanding of the wrong done by intolerance, and a different conception of the limitations of toleration. It is not justified because we are all separate free choosers, but because we are interdependent victims. It is not limited by the desire to facilitate autonomy for each, but by the larger desire to secure a sense of belonging for all. This latter is a more dangerous desire than any the liberal countenances, but it is, I believe, the desire which goes unfulfilled in liberal answers to questions of toleration.

Guide to Further Reading

Discussions of toleration rarely form the central theme of modern books in political philosophy, but reference to the topic is made by many writers on related topics, particularly those writing within the liberal tradition. The most accessible and sustained modern account of toleration is King (1976), and the most stimulating pieces are to be found in Wolff *et al.* (1965), which includes Marcuse's seminal essay 'Repressive Tolerance'. A useful account of religious toleration and its relationship to pluralism and relativism is Newman (1982). These aside, readers interested in toleration are best advised to go back to some of the classic texts – particularly Locke's *Letter on Toleration* and Mill's *On Liberty*. They should also refer to Rawls (1971), Dworkin (1977, 1985), and Raz (1986), where theories of toleration are presented as part of liberal political theory.

I have divided the guide to further reading into three sections: the first recommends some criticisms and discussions of John Locke's *Letter on Toleration*. The second suggests some commentaries on John Stuart Mill's *On Liberty*. The third indicates some modern works where the concept of toleration is discussed.

Locke's *Letter on Toleration*

Although Locke's political philosophy has received extensive commentary, there has been comparatively little philosophical interest in the *Letter*. Dunn (1984) provides an excellent short account of Locke's philosophical thought, emphasising the role of the political philosophy. Ashcraft (1986) gives a very detailed examination of the historical circumstances which influenced Locke's political philosophy. He discusses the *Letter* itself, as well as a whole range of related writings and correspondence. The philosophical implications of the *Letter* are lucidly discussed by Waldron (1988) and Cranston (1987).

Mill's *On Liberty*

The literature on Mill's *On Liberty* is huge. A very useful introductory book is Thomas (1985). For more detailed criticism, readers should consult Himmelfarb (1974), Gray (1983) and Rees (1985). Rees provides an excellent account of the nineteenth-century reception of *On Liberty* and also makes telling criticisms of Himmelfarb's version of the 'two Mills' thesis. However, his most important contribution to the debate is his interpretation of Mill's principle and its distinction between self-regarding and other-regarding actions. Gray's book wrestles with the thorny problem of Mill's utilitarianism, and concludes that the liberty principle is itself an application of the principle of utility.

Modern writings

One of the most stimulating contributions is Raz (1986). The final chapters provide a convincing defence of a theory of toleration founded on the value of autonomy. Elements of this defence are also to be found in Raz (1982, 1988).

Over the years Ronald Dworkin has written extensively about practical problems of toleration. Many of his most important articles (on pornography, racial equality and civil disobedience) are now collected together in Dworkin (1985). These articles discuss the foundation of liberalism in a principle of equal concern and respect. They also examine the practical consequences which Dworkin believes to follow from such liberalism.

A useful general book on liberalism is Arblaster (1984). Articles on toleration in the history of political theory are gathered together in Mendus (1988).

Bibliography

Ackerman, B. A. (1980) *Social Justice in the Liberal State* (Yale University Press).

Arblaster, A. (1984) *The Rise and Decline of Western Liberalism* (Blackwell, Oxford).

Ashcraft, R. (1986) *Revolutionary Politics and Locke's 'Two Treatises of Government'* (Princeton University Press).

Barry, B. (1965) *Political Argument* (Routledge & Kegan Paul, London).

Bates, M. S. (1945) *Religious Liberty: An Inquiry* (International Missionary Council, New York).

Benyon, J. (ed.) (1984) *Scarman and After: Essays Reflecting on Lord Scarman's Report, the riots and their aftermath* (Pergamon, London).

Berlin, I. (1969) *Four Essays on Liberty* (Clarendon, Oxford).

Bossy, J. (1985) *Christianity in the West 1400–1700* (Oxford University Press).

Burgess, A. (1984) *Ninety Nine Novels: The Best in English since 1939* (Allison and Busby, London).

Cooper, D. (1983) 'The Free Man' in A. Phillips Griffiths (ed.) *Of Liberty*, Royal Institute of Philosophy Lecture Series: 15 (Cambridge University Press).

Cranston, M. (1987) 'John Locke and the Case for Toleration' in S. Mendus and D. Edwards (eds) *On Toleration* (Clarendon, Oxford).

Dunn, J. (1969) *Political Thought of John Locke* (Cambridge University Press).

Dunn, J. (1984) *Locke* (Oxford University Press).

Dunn, J. (1985) *Rethinking Modern Political Theory* (Cambridge University Press).

Dworkin, A. (1981) *Pornography: Men Possessing Women* (Women's Press, London).

Dworkin, R. (1977) *Taking Rights Seriously* (Duckworth, London).

Dworkin, R. (1983) 'What Liberalism Isn't', *New York Review of Books*, January.

Dworkin, R. (1985) *A Matter of Principle* (Harvard University Press, Cambridge, Mass.).

Eccleshall, R. *et al.* (1984) *Political Ideologies: An Introduction* (Hutchinson, London).

Edwards, D. S. (1985) 'Toleration and the English Law of Blasphemy' in

J. Horton and S. Mendus (eds) *Aspects of Toleration* (Methuen, London).

Gentile, G. (1960) *Genesis and Structure of Society* (Illinois University Press, Urbana).

Gray, J. (1983) *Mill on Liberty: A Defence* (Routledge and Kegan Paul, London).

Himmelfarb, G. (1974) *Of Liberty and Liberalism* (Borzoi Books, Knopf, New York).

Horton, J. (1985) 'Toleration, Morality and Harm' in Horton and Mendus (eds) *Aspects of Toleration* (Methuen, London).

Horton, J. and Mendus, S. (eds) (1985) *Aspects of Toleration* (Methuen, London).

Hume, D. (1975) *A Treatise of Human Nature*, L. A. Selby-Bigge (ed.) (Clarendon, Oxford).

Jones, P. (1989) 'The Ideal of the Neutral State' in R. Goodin and A. Reeve (eds) *Liberal Neutrality* (Routledge, London).

Kant, I. (1949) 'What is Orientation in Thinking?', in L. W. Beck (trans. and ed.) *Kant's Critique of Practical Reason and Other Writings in Moral Philosophy* (Chicago University Press).

Kant, I. (1966) *Groundwork for a Metaphysic of Morals*, trans. H. J. Paton as *The Moral Law* (Hutchinson, London).

Kant, I. (1968) *Critique of Pure Reason*, J. Kemp Smith (ed. and trans.) (Macmillan, London).

Kappeler, S. (1986) *The Pornography of Representation* (Polity Press, Oxford, Cambridge).

Kelly, P. (1984) *John Locke: Authority, Conscience and Religious Toleration* (M. A. Dissertation, University of York).

Kerner (1968) *Report of the National Advisory Commission on Civil Disorders* (Bantam Books, New York).

King, P. (1976) *Toleration* (George Allen and Unwin, London).

Locke, J. (1983) *A Letter Concerning Toleration*, Tully, J. (ed.) (Hackett, Indianapolis).

Mazlish, B. (1975) *James and John Stuart Mill* (Basic Books, New York).

Mendus, S. (1985) 'Harm, Offence and Censorship' in Horton and Mendus (eds) *Aspects of Toleration* (Methuen, London).

Mendus, S. and Edwards, D. (1987) *On Toleration* (Clarendon Press, Oxford).

Mendus, S. (1988) *Justifying Toleration: Conceptual and Historical Perspectives* (Cambridge University Press).

Mill, J. S. (1984) *Essays on Equality, Law and Education*, Collected Works, Vol. XXI (University of Toronto Press).

Mill, J. S. (1962) *Utilitarianism*, M. Warnock (ed.) (Fontana, London).

Mill, J. S. (1962) 'Bentham', M. Warnock (ed.) *Utilitarianism* (Fontana, London).

Mill, J. S. (1983) *The Subjection of Women*, K. Soper (ed.) (Virago, London).

Mill, J. S. (1978) *On Liberty* (Penguin, Harmondsworth). ed. G. Himmelfarb.

Mill, J. S. (1973) *A System of Logic*, in *Collected Works* Vol. VIII (University of Toronto Press).

Miller, D. (1988) 'Socialism and Toleration' in Mendus (ed.) *Justifying Toleration: Conceptual and Historical Perspectives* (Cambridge University Press).

Murdoch, I. (1961) 'Against Dryness' in *Encounter*.

Newman, J. (1982) *Foundations of Religious Tolerance* (University of Toronto Press).

Nicholson, P. (1985) 'Toleration as a Moral Ideal' in Horton and Mendus (eds) *Aspects of Toleration* (Methuen, London).

Packe, M. St John (1954) *The Life of John Stuart Mill* (Secker and Warburg, London).

Passmore, J. A. (1986) 'Locke and the Ethics of Belief' in Anthony Kenny (ed.) *Rationalism, Empiricism and Idealism*, British Academy Lectures on the History of Philosophy (Clarendon, Oxford).

Pateman, C. (1984) 'The Shame of the Marriage Contract' in J. Stiehm (ed.) *Women's View of the Political World of Men* (Dobbs Ferry Transnational Publishers, New York).

Pateman, C. (1988) *The Sexual Contract* (Polity Press, Oxford, Cambridge).

Pelczynski, Z. and Gray, J. (1984) *Conceptions of Liberty in Political Philosophy* (Athlone, London).

Phillips, A. (1984) 'Fraternity', in B. Pimlott (ed.) *Fabian Essays in Socialist Thought* (Heinemann, London).

Phillips Griffiths, A. (1983) *Of Liberty*, Royal Institute of Philosophy Lecture Series: 15 (Cambridge University Press).

Raphael, D. D. (1988) 'The Intolerable', in S. Mendus (ed.) *Justifying Toleration: Conceptual and Historical Perspectives* (Cambridge University Press).

Rawls, J. (1971) *A Theory of Justice* (Oxford University Press).

Raz, J. (1982) 'Liberalism, Autonomy, and the Politics of Neutral Concern' *Mid-West Studies in Philosophy*, 7, pp.89–120.

Raz, J. (1986) *The Morality of Freedom* (Clarendon, Oxford).

Raz, J. (1988) 'Autonomy, Toleration and the Harm Principle' in S. Mendus (ed.) *Justifying Toleration: Conceptual and Historical Perspectives* (Cambridge University Press).

Rees, J. C. (1985) *John Stuart Mill's 'On Liberty'* (Clarendon Press, Oxford).

Robson, J. (1968) *The Improvement of Mankind* (University of Toronto Press).

Sandel, M. (1982) *Liberalism and the Limits of Justice* (Cambridge University Press).

Sandel, M. (ed.) (1984) *Liberalism and its Critics* (Blackwell, Oxford).

Scarman, L. (1986) *The Scarman Report: The Brixton Disorders, 10–12 April, 1981* (Penguin, Harmondsworth).

Scarman, L. (1987) 'Toleration and the Law' in S. Mendus and D. Edwards (eds) *On Toleration* (Oxford University Press).

Smith, G. W. (1984) 'J. S. Mill on Freedom' in Z. Pelczynski and J. Gray (eds) *Conceptions of Liberty in Political Philosophy* (Athlone, London).

Stephen, J. Fitzjames (1967) *Liberty, Equality, Fraternity* (Cambridge University Press).

Taylor, C. (1979) 'What's Wrong with Negative Liberty?' in A. Ryan (ed.) *The Idea of Freedom: Essay in Honour of Isaiah Berlin* (Oxford University Press).

Thomas, W. (1985) *Mill* (Oxford University Press).

Tuck, R. (1988) 'Scepticism and Toleration in the Seventeenth Century' in S. Mendus (ed.) *Justifying Toleration* (Cambridge University Press).

Tully, J. H. (1983) *John Locke: A Letter Concerning Toleration* (Hackett, Indianapolis).

Waldron, J. (1987) 'Theoretical Foundations of Liberalism' *Philosophical Quarterly*, 37, 147, pp.127–50.

Waldron, J. (1988) 'Locke, Toleration and the Rationality of Persecution' in S. Mendus (ed.) *Justifying Toleration: Conceptual and Historical Perspectives* (Cambridge University Press).

Warnock, M. (1987) 'The Limits of Toleration' in S. Mendus and D. Edwards (eds) *On Toleration* (Oxford University Press).

Weale, A. (1985) 'Toleration, Individual Differences and Respect for Persons' in J. Horton and S. Mendus (eds) *Aspects of Toleration* (Methuen, London).

Williams, B. (1973) *Problems of the Self* (Cambridge University Press).

Williams, B. (1985) *Ethics and the Limits of Philosophy* (Fontana, London).

Wolff, R. P. *et al.* (1965) *A Critique of Pure Tolerance* (Beacon Press, Boston).

Index

169